The Return and Reign
of Jesus Christ

The Return and Reign of Jesus Christ

by
John MacArthur, Jr.

WORD OF GRACE COMMUNICATIONS
P.O. Box 4000
Panorama City, CA 91412

ISBN: 0-8024-5358-9

1 2 3 4 5 6 7 8 Printing/LC/Year 93 92 91 90 89 88

Contents

These Bible studies are taken from messages delivered by Pastor-Teacher John MacArthur, Jr., at Grace Community Church in Panorama City, California. These messages have been combined into an 8-tape album entitled *The Return and Reign of Jesus Christ*. You may purchase this series either in an attractive vinyl cassette album or as individual cassettes. To purchase these tapes, request the album *The Return and Reign of Jesus Christ*, or ask for the tapes by their individual GC numbers. Please consult the current price list; then, send your order, making your check payable to:

WORD OF GRACE COMMUNICATIONS
P.O. Box 4000
Panorama City, CA 91412

Or call the following toll-free number:
1-800-55-GRACE

1

The Saga of Two Conquerors—Part 1

Outline

Introduction
A. The Signs of the Times
B. The Setting of the Scene
    1. The purpose of Zechariah's prophecy
    2. The pledge of God's promise

Lesson
I. The Human Conqueror (vv. 1-8)
    A. The Purging by God (vv. 1-7)
        1. Of Syria (vv. 1-2a)
            a) The places of judgment (v. 1a)
            b) The perspective of judgment (vv. 1b-2a)
        2. Of Tyre (vv. 2b-4)
            a) Her pride (vv. 2b-3)
            b) Her prince (Ezek. 28)
            c) Her punishment (v. 4)
        3. Of Philistia (vv. 5-7)
            a) A frightful retribution (v. 5)
            b) A foreign raid (v. 6)
            c) A faithful remnant (v. 7)
    B. The Protection by God (v. 8)
        1. In the days of Alexander (v. 8a)
        2. At the return of Christ (v. 8b)

Introduction

As Christians we believe that Jesus Christ, the Messiah of Israel and Savior of the world, is going to return to earth to establish the kingdom promised to Israel and all those who have trusted in Him. We anticipate the time when the Adamic curse will be reversed and the earth will be recreated. Jesus Christ will reign as King of kings and Lord of lords.

Many of the details of that coming kingdom and Christ's return are given in Scripture. In fact, a major element of Old Testament prophecy is of the coming kingdom. The prophets frequently foretold the ending of history, the judgment of the nations, and the reign of Messiah, thus fulfilling promises made to David (2 Sam. 7:12) and to Abraham (Gen. 12:1-3). The Messiah will come not only to conquer the nations who oppose God but also to redeem Israel and establish the kingdom into which all believing saints of all the ages will be ushered. Similarly, the New Testament is full of statements asserting that "the Lord is at hand" (Phil. 4:5) and "it is the last time" (1 John 2:18).

A. The Signs of the Times

Christians have always believed they were living in the time of Christ's return. However, things happening today make it reasonable to believe that His return is close. For example, Ezekiel 39 speaks of the great battle of Armageddon, which will occur at the end of the Tribulation, right before the Lord returns to establish His kingdom. All the nations of the world will be at war, yet Christ will defeat them all. Warfare of such magnitude would have been hard for the people of that day to imagine.

Ezekiel 39:1-10 says, "Prophesy against Gog, and say, Thus saith the Lord God: Behold, I am against thee, O Gog, the chief prince of Meshech and Tubal, and I will turn thee back, and leave but the sixth part of thee" (vv. 1-2). That may well be a reference to a Soviet army descending from the north upon Israel. God will almost totally destroy it. Verses 4-5 say, "Thou shalt fall upon the mountains of Israel, thou, and all thy hordes, and the peoples that are with thee; I will give thee unto the ravenous birds of every sort, and to the beasts of the field to be devoured. Thou shalt fall upon the open field; for I have spoken it, saith the Lord God."

Ravenous birds will devour the carcasses of the northern army. In Revelation 19:18-19, a comparative passage in the

New Testament, God calls the ravenous birds to come and feed on "the flesh of the kings, and the flesh of captains, and the flesh of mighty men" who will have been slain in that great battle.

B. The Setting of the Scene

Zechariah 9-14 foretells the downfall of the nations, the salvation of Israel, and the establishment of the Messiah as King. Chapters 9-14 are divided into two parts: chapters 9-11 deal with the destruction of the nations and the rise of Israel, and chapters 12-14 emphasize the spiritual restoration of Israel. And although we see salvation of Israel in the first section, its main emphasis is on the political scene.

Zechariah was the grandson of Iddo, who had returned to Jerusalem with 43,000 of the children of Israel in 538 B.C. under Zerubbabel, following the seventy-year captivity of Israel in Babylon (Ezra 2:64; Neh. 12:4, 6; Zech. 1:1). The former glory of Israel was only a memory. Although the people had begun to rebuild their cities, the work came to a halt. The surrounding nations posed a threat to the Jews, who were unable to defend themselves against an attack. Therefore God encouraged them to rebuild Jerusalem and trust Him to protect them by sending the prophets Haggai and Zechariah.

1. The purpose of Zechariah's prophecy

Zechariah begins his prophecy of encouragement to Israel, saying, "The Lord answered the angel that talked with me with good words and comforting words. . . . Cry yet, saying, Thus saith the Lord of hosts: My cities through prosperity shall yet be spread abroad, and the Lord shall yet comfort Zion, and shall yet choose Jerusalem" (1:13, 17). Zechariah's message was a comforting message, like that of Isaiah, who said, "Comfort ye, comfort ye my people, saith your God" (Isa. 40:1). Although the great and glorious city of Jerusalem was in ruins, God would inspire and enable them to restore it. That was the message of the first eight chapters.

The rest of the book focuses on the future. Rather than the immediate rebuilding of Jerusalem in his own time,

Zechariah envisions the great restoration of God's kingdom in the end times. He takes a giant step from his own time to the fulfillment of prophecy at the end of the ages. However, the two parts of this book are connected with the theme of God's love for Israel and His faithfulness to fulfill His promise to His people—not only to rebuild Israel historically but to establish His victorious reign in the end times.

2. The pledge of God's promise

God's promise of a temporal restoration of Jerusalem was fulfilled a few decades after Zechariah's time. But that was only a pledge of what God was planning to do in the end. It was simply a way to prove to His people that He meant to keep His promises. The Jewish person could recall how God restored his capital city and be confident that He would keep His Word in the future. Frequently in the Old Testament, when God gave a prophecy regarding the distant future, He also gave a short-term prophecy with a closer historical fulfillment. It served as a signpost to the greater fulfillment in the future. Such a pattern instilled confidence that what was prophesied would surely happen in the future. The historical fulfillment was God's tangible token of His promise. For example, Daniel prophesied about the Antichrist in the end times, and the closer historical representation was fulfilled by a king named Antiochus Epiphanes (cf. 11:21-35). Antiochus was given in the prophecy as a signpost of the Antichrist.

In the same way, chapter 9 distinguishes between two conquerors. The first conqueror (vv. 1-8) was the closer historical fulfillment of the second conqueror, who is yet to come (vv. 9-17). The first conqueror's name is not given in the text, but from the circumstances described he is obviously Alexander the Great. He was an unrighteous pagan used by God to destroy the nations and preserve Israel. He is a human picture of Christ returning to judge the nations and save Israel at the end of the Tribulation. The implication is that if God can do such works through a godless human, imagine what He will do in the end times through the Divine Conqueror when He comes!

10

Lesson

I. THE HUMAN CONQUEROR (vv. 1-8)

A. The Purging by God (vv. 1-7)

1. Of Syria (vv. 1-2*a*)

a) The places of judgment (v. 1*a*)

"The burden of the word of the Lord in the land of Hadrach, and Damascus shall be its rest."

"Burden" (Heb., *massa*), coming from a Hebrew verb meaning "to take or lift up," came to be used of a prophetical message of judgment. It was like a great burden on the back of a prophet.

This particular judgment coming from the "word of the Lord" was directed to the land of Hadrach, an obscure place that is not easily identified. Some believe it was the ancient village of Hatarika, near Damascus, which was northeast of the Sea of Galilee and mentioned in the annals of the Assyrian kings.

Another explanation is that it refers to the Medo-Persian kingdom. H. C. Leupold in his *Exposition of Zechariah* notes that the components of Hadrach, *had* ("sharp") and *rakh* ("soft"), may well be a reference to the dual Medo-Persian kingdom in Zechariah's day ([Grand Rapids: Baker, 1971], pp. 164-65). Its leaders were aggressive conquerors, sharp like swords yet soft from debauchery. Therefore Hadrach may have been a veiled reference to the Medo-Persian Empire to protect Israel from inciting the anger of that empire.

Verse 1 also refers to Damascus, one of the oldest cities in the world. This ancient capital of Syria was one of Israel's worst enemies from 900 to 721 B.C. It was several hundred years later that Alexander came into the picture. At the battle of Issus in southeast Asia Minor in 333 B.C., Alexander defeated Darius, king of

11

Persia, and began to break the back of the Medo-Persian Empire. That defeat opened the door to Syria (north of Palestine), Phoenicia and Philistia (along its coast), and Egypt (south of it) in his campaign to conquer the great powers of the world. The Holy Spirit used Zechariah to reveal Alexander's battle plan centuries before Alexander was born!

b) The perspective of judgment (vv. 1b-2a)

"When the eyes of man, as of all the tribes of Israel, shall be toward the Lord. And Hamath also shall border by it."

Zechariah was saying that God's judgment would be visible to all mankind, especially Israel. Their focus would be "toward the Lord," as they fixed their fearful gaze on Alexander, who would be the instrument of the Lord. The inhabitants of Israel and the Gentile nations of Syria (including Hamath, a neighboring city of Syria and the site of modern Hama), Phoenicia, Philistia, and Egypt were shaking in their boots. Without knowing it, they were witnessing the Lord coming in judgment through that Greek conqueror.

Throughout history God has used ungodly people to carry out His judgment. In the book of Habakkuk God used the Chaldeans as His instruments. Isaiah prophesied about Cyrus, the king of the Medes, whom God used to lead many of the Jews from Babylon to Israel (Isa. 45:1-4). God even used Herod Antipas to bring about the death of Christ (cf. Acts 4:27; Luke 23:11-12), the act that brought about the redemption of mankind. God has often used pagans to bring about His judgment. Alexander the Great was no exception; he was simply doing what God appointed him to do. Zechariah 9:4 says, "Behold, the Lord will cast her [the city of Tyre] out." Rather than mentioning Alexander, it states that God would overthrow the city. Bible commentaries identify this passage as referring to Alexander the Great because it so precisely follows the order of his campaign. But he merely foreshadowed the conquest of the nations by the final Divine Conqueror.

12

2. Of Tyre (vv. 2b-4)

a) Her pride (vv. 2b-3)

"Tyre, and Sidon, though it be very wise. And Tyre did build herself a stronghold, and heaped up silver like the dust, and fine gold like the mire of the streets."

The end of verse 2 mentions that judgment will also fall upon Tyre and Sidon, whose only significance was its proximity to Tyre, the prominent city of Phoenicia. That nation had made great maritime and mercantile accomplishments and was therefore proud. Their worldly wisdom led them to believe that they were invincible.

A couple centuries before Alexander arrived on the scene, Tyre had been conquered by the Babylonians. As a result, they moved their city from the mainland to an island a half mile offshore. Although small, the island was seemingly impenetrable. "Tyre [Heb., *tsor*, "rock"] did build herself a stronghold [Heb., *matsor*, "citadel"]" is a play on words in the Hebrew text, using similar sounding words. The new Tyre was built on a fortified rock, having a 150-foot wall around the entire island. Because of their offshore location and the unsurpassed Phoenician navy to defend them, the people of Tyre believed they were invincible.

b) Her prince (Ezek. 28)

Ezekiel 28 tells us what a vile city Tyre was, as the prophet pronounces judgment upon its king: "The word of the Lord came again unto me, saying, Son of man, say unto the prince of Tyre, Thus saith the Lord God: Because thine heart is lifted up, and thou hast said, I am a god, I sit in the seat of God, in the midst of the seas, yet thou art a man, and not God, though thou set thine heart as the heart of God" (vv. 1-2). The prince of Tyre had an ego problem: he believed he was God and assumed he was invincible. As Ezekiel condemns the pride of this king, he makes a dramatic change in verse 11 to the ultimate motivation and source of evil behind him: "Moreover, the word of the Lord came unto me, saying, Son of man, take up a lamentation upon the king of Tyre, and say unto him, Thus saith the Lord God: Thou sealest up the sum, full of wisdom, and perfect in beauty. Thou hast been in Eden, the garden of God; every precious stone was thy covering. . . . Thou art the anointed cherub that covereth, and I have set thee so; thou wast on the holy mountain of God; thou hast walked up and down in the midst of the stones of fire. Thou wast perfect in thy ways from the day that thou wast created, till iniquity was found in thee" (vv. 13-15). That description of a perfect and beautiful being who once resided in heaven and in the Garden of Eden can be of none other than Satan.

c) Her punishment (v. 4)

"Behold, the Lord will cast her out, and he will smite her power in the sea, and she shall be devoured with fire."

Every detail in that verse was accomplished by Alexander the Great. During his campaign in Palestine he requested supplies from Tyre. When they refused to assist him, his army took the rubble that was left from the ancient city of Tyre, threw it into the sea to build a half-mile causeway, marched out to the island fortress, and defeated the city with the assistance of the navies of surrounding nations. Alexander did in seven months what the Assyrian king Shalmaneser IV couldn't do in five years, or the Babylonian king Nebuchadnezzar in thirteen years. But because it was time for God's judgment, the city came crashing down. Today there is nothing of any significance on the ancient site of Tyre.

Through Zechariah God is saying He will judge the nations in the future through the Messiah. The historical illustration of how He destroyed one of the most fortified, impregnable cities in the world is only a small token of what He will do when Christ returns. The historical fulfillment concerning Alexander the Great was a confirmation that God will keep His promise concerning His messianic kingdom.

3. Of Philistia (vv. 5-7)

   a) A frightful retribution (v. 5)

   "Ashkelon shall see it, and fear; Gaza also shall see it, and be very sorrowful, and Ekron; for her expectations shall be ashamed; and the king shall perish from Gaza, and Ashkelon shall not be inhabited."

   Moving south, Alexander next came to Philistia. By then the Philistines were terrified. They had watched Alexander wipe out the Medo-Persian army in the battle of Issus, sweep with lightning swiftness to Syria to the east, and then advance on Phoenicia in the south, decimating an impregnable fortress in seven months. Now that he was heading further south, they panicked—with good reason.

   Alexander's defeat of Gaza is recorded in detail by first-century Greek historian Arrian in *The Campaigns of Alexander* (2.27). Whereas all the other cities of Philistia were conquered easily because they feared Alexander, Gaza resisted him for five months before they surrendered. As a result, Alexander refused to give the people of Gaza the semi-independence he allowed the other cities he conquered. Curtius, the Latin biographer of Alexander, tells us he had their king, Batis, dragged through the streets of the city until dead (4.6.29). It is amazing that Zechariah's prophecy was given hundreds of years before Alexander was born.

   b) A foreign raid (v. 6)

   "A bastard [Heb., *mamzer*, "foreigner," "mongrel"] shall dwell in Ashdod, and I will cut off the pride of the Philistines."

   The prediction was that the Philistines would lose their country to foreigners or scavengers because

15

they were proud. God broke their pride with Alexander. Today there are no Philistines.

c) A faithful remnant (v. 7)

"I will take away his blood out of his mouth, and his abominations from between his teeth; but he that remaineth, even he, shall be for our God, and he shall be like a governor in Judah, and Ekron like a Jebusite."

In spite of the terrible destruction of the Philistines, there was evidence of God's grace. God's judgment was a purging of the Philistines' idolatry. The Philistine nation is pictured as a man participating in the idolatrous blood sacrifices of pagan worship (cf. Acts 15:20; 1 Cor. 8:4). The divinely designed conquest by Alexander would put an end to their idolatry and cause the remaining Philistines to repent and turn to God.

Remembering the Righteous Remnant

In any time of God's judgment, there's always a place for the repentant. When the prophet Malachi pronounced judgment upon Judah, some faithful Israelites gathered together and prayed. As a result, "a book of remembrance was written before him [God] for them that feared the Lord" (3:16). The Lord assured them, saying, "They shall be mine . . . in that day when I make up my jewels" (v. 17). God always remembers the repentant, no matter what the circumstances of judgment.

Zechariah prophesied that the Philistine who turned to God would have as many privileges as a governor over Judah. What a tremendous privilege for a Gentile! God didn't say, "Because you were pagans and not Israelites, you are second-class citizens." No. Even though they were formerly pagans, some of the Philistines would be uniquely exalted by God. Those Philistines, symbolized by the city of Ekron, would become like the Jebusites. They were the inhabitants of Jerusalem before David made it his capital. Some of them, like Araunah, whom David respected (2 Sam. 24:15-25), came to believe in the true God and remained in the city.

B. The Protection by God (v. 8)

1. In the days of Alexander (v. 8*a*)

"I will encamp about mine house because of the army, because of him that passeth by, and because of him that returneth."

Having conquered Philistia, Alexander's next stop was Jerusalem. But God promised that He would protect His dwelling place. The first part of verse 8 precisely describes Alexander's advance against Jerusalem as recorded in *Antiquities of the Jews* (11.8.3-5), by Josephus, the ancient Jewish historian. Alexander would never conquer Jerusalem because God would encamp around it and protect it.

Alexander sent word to Jaddua, the high priest at that time, to pay tribute to him. But the nation was already paying tribute to the king of Persia, and Jaddua refused to break his allegiance to that nation. Alexander became enraged and planned to destroy Jerusalem when he had finished his conquest of the Philistine cities. The high priest called the people of Jerusalem to sacrifice to God and pray for deliverance. According to Josephus, God gave the high priest a dream, instructing him to welcome Alexander outside the city when he arrived.

When Alexander and his army marched to the city, the high priest, arrayed in purple and scarlet with a miter on his head and carrying a gold plate with God's name engraved on it, led a procession of priests dressed in white. When the conqueror saw this, he saluted the high priest and honored the name of God, saying he had seen a person like the high priest in a dream while in Macedonia. Therefore he treated Jerusalem with kindness and headed on to Egypt. And as Zechariah prophesied, he returned through Palestine without harming Jerusalem or its inhabitants. Alexander judged the nations but he honored the city of Jerusalem

17

through the intervention of God. If God can use a pagan king to judge the ungodly and to preserve His people in such a miraculous way, imagine what He can do with a divine King whose judgment will be all the greater and who will actually deliver His people! This King of the future is Christ.

2. At the return of Christ (v. 8*b*)

"No oppressor shall pass through them any more; for now I have seen with mine eyes."

Here Zechariah prophecies a supernatural and lasting protection that can refer only to the protection provided at the second coming of Christ. The Holy Spirit takes us suddenly from Alexander to Jesus Christ. When Christ returns to judge the nations and deliver His people, no nation will ever oppress them again. "I have seen with mine eyes" tells us that God has witnessed all the affliction Israel has encountered and promises peace through the Messiah, the Prince of Peace.

The human conqueror Alexander was a signpost. His temporary fulfillment of prophecy encourages us to keep our eyes on the greater fulfillment to come. Christ will come again and judge the nations in a way infinitely greater than anything Alexander dreamed of—with might and power beyond the conception of any man. As the whole earth falls under His judgment, God will preserve His people, as Alexander spared them in his day. But He will go far beyond the works of that human conqueror to restore Israel and give them their long-awaited kingdom.

Focusing on the Facts

1. Why must the Messiah return (see p. 8)?
2. What is the battle of Armageddon (see p. 8)?
3. What does Zechariah 9-14 foretell (see p. 9)?
4. Why did God need to encourage the Jewish remnant of Zechariah's day? How did He do that (see p. 9)?

5. How is the focus of Zechariah's message in chapter 9-14 different from the preceding chapters? What theme connects both parts of the book (see pp. 9-10)?
6. God's promise of a temporal restoration of Jerusalem was a pledge of what? Explain (see p. 10).
7. Give an example of a prophecy with a short-term fulfillment that has a greater fulfillment in the future (see p. 10).
8. Identify the two conquerors in view in chapter 9. The first is a historical illustration of whom (see p. 10)?
9. To what did Alexander's defeat of the Persian army at Issus lead (see pp. 11-12)?
10. In what way were the people seeing the Lord in the conquests of Alexander (vv. 1, 4; see p. 12)?
11. What did Tyre assume about itself? Why (see p. 13)?
12. Identify the source of evil behind the prince of Tyre. Support your answer with Scripture (see pp. 13-14).
13. How did God execute judgment on the seemingly invincible city of Tyre? That is a historical illustration of what (see p. 14)?
14. How was Zechariah's prophecy concerning Gath's sorrow and her king precisely fulfilled (v. 5; see p. 15)?
15. In breaking the pride of the Philistines, how did God then demonstrate His grace (see p. 16)?
16. Explain the significance of a faithful Philistine being treated like a Jebusite (see pp. 16-17)?
17. What prophecy did Zechariah give concerning Jerusalem (vv. 7-8; see p. 17)?
18. Knowing that oppressors did in fact pass through Jerusalem after Alexander, the promise of the second half of verse 8 must refer to what (see p. 18)?
19. Explain how Christ's judgment of the nations and dealings with Israel will be different from Alexander's (see p. 18).

Pondering the Principles

1. Prophecy has the practical effect of increasing our faith and giving us hope. Its fulfillment demonstrates the faithfulness of God and shows He can be trusted in other areas. Imagine the increased confidence the inhabitants of Jerusalem must have had in God when they realized that their lives had been preserved in

fulfillment of a prophecy given about two hundred years before! Consider the hope they would have experienced when they understood that it meant a glorious future awaited them. Are you letting fulfilled prophecy build your faith in God and hope in the future? Several books have been written that discuss how biblical prophecies have been specifically fulfilled (for example, Josh McDowell's *Evidence That Demands a Verdict* [San Bernardino, Calif.: Here's Life, 1979]). You might read one of them or use a conservative commentary to study a specific prophecy such as Daniel 9:24-27. Praise God for His faithfulness and thank Him for the hope He has provided for those who know and love Him.

2. It is easy to assume that people who worship other gods are past the point of repentance. But that is a false assumption. God led the pagan city of Nineveh to repent through the preaching of Jonah. Zechariah told us about the faithful remnant of Philistines who would be respected by the Jewish people. Read the short prophecy of Jonah, meditating on God's grace. Endeavor to be an instrument of His mercy toward others.

2
The Saga of Two Conquerors—Part 2

Outline

Introduction
A. The Results of the King's Return
B. The Reasons for the King's Return
   1. Symbolized
   2. Specified
      a) Judgment
      b) Salvation
         (1) Luke 21:27-28
         (2) Romans 11:26-27
         (3) Jeremiah 31:3-4

Review
I. The Human Conqueror (vv. 1-8)
   A. The Purging by God (vv. 1-7)
   B. The Protection by God (v. 8)

Lesson
II. The Divine Conqueror (vv. 9-17)
   A. His Character (v. 9)
      1. He is King
      2. He is just
      3. He is Savior
      4. He is meek
         a) The general fulfillment of Christ's lowliness
         b) The specific fulfillment of Zechariah's prophecy
            (1) The request of the Prince
            (2) The reaffirmation of the prophecy
            (3) The reception of the people

B. His Conquest (vv. 10-15)
    1. The reign of peace (v. 10)
    2. The ratification of the promise (v. 11*a*)
    3. The release of the prisoners (v. 11*b*)
    4. The resource of the prisoners (v. 12)
    5. The rebellion of the people (v. 13)
    6. The rebellion as a preview (v. 14)
    7. The resource of protection (v. 15*a*)
    8. The rejoicing of the people (v. 15*b*)
C. His Care (vv. 16-17)
    1. The redemption of the remnant (v. 16)
    2. The response of the redeemed (v. 17)

Conclusion

Introduction

A. The Results of the King's Return

People often ask, "What's wrong with the world? Why are
there such things as injustice, turmoil, conflict, disease,
pain, tragedy, and chaos?" The answer is simple: the King
is absent. As the Messiah of Israel, He came once and
promised to right the world. Although He was rejected as
the King of Israel (John 19:14-15), He will return again as
the Prince of Peace (Isa. 9:6) and the "King of kings, and
Lord of lords" (Rev. 19:16). He is going to take back this
world from Satan, the usurper, who has had it for a long
time (John 12:31; 2 Cor. 4:4; Eph. 2:2; 1 John 5:19; Rev.
12:9). When the King comes back, war, injustice, and an-
archy will end; pain and disease will be brought to a minimum in His kingdom. He will seize the reins of the world's
governments and rule with firmness and compassion.

B. The Reasons for the King's Return

We find two elements to Christ's return: one is positive—
salvation—and one is negative—the judgment associated
with His return.

1. Symbolized

   In Revelation 10:8-10 John says, "The voice which I heard from heaven spoke unto me again, and said, Go and take the little scroll which is open in the hand of the angel who standeth upon the sea and upon the earth. And I went unto the angel, and said unto him, Give me the little scroll. And he said unto me, Take it, and eat it up; and it shall make thy belly bitter, but it shall be in thy mouth sweet as honey. And I took the little scroll out of the angel's hand, and ate it up; and it was in my mouth sweet as honey, and as soon as I had eaten it, my belly was bitter." This followed John's vision of Christ's returning with the title deed to the earth. John experienced it as being sweet because of the wrongs that are righted, the salvation that comes about for Israel and an innumerable amount of Gentiles, and the honor given to Christ as He establishes His kingdom. But John then experienced the bitterness of judgment as people are eternally damned and nations are destroyed for their rejection of Jesus Christ. Like John we may have that mixed reaction. We rejoice in His salvation but are disheartened by the judgment that awaits the world.

2. Specified

   In the last five chapters of Zechariah, we find those same two elements emphasized: the salvation of Israel and the restoration of the earth and the fearful judgments that fall. In contrast to His first coming, when evil men succeeded in killing Him, He will destroy His enemies at His second coming. Only after judgment will He begin healing a sick world and allowing the wonders of His salvation to come to pass.

   a) Judgment

      God's judgment is not easy to comprehend. Isaiah 28:21 calls it "his strange work" because it seems contrary to His love. However, God's judgment is inextricably linked with His love—He loves so much He protects us from evil forever. The only way He can do that is to destroy evil and those who have rejected His grace.

The Bible is filled with oracles of judgment, especially in the major and minor prophets. For example, Joel 3:12-16 says, "Let the nations be wakened, and come up to the Valley of Jehoshaphat [the valley created when Christ returns to the Mount of Olives]; for there will I sit to judge all the nations round about. Put in the sickle; for the harvest is ripe; come, get down; for the press is full, the vats overflow; for their wickedness is great. Multitudes, multitudes in the valley of decision; for the day of the Lord is near in the valley of decision. The sun and the moon shall be darkened, and the stars shall withdraw their shining. The Lord also shall roar out of Zion, and utter his voice from Jerusalem, and the heavens and the earth shall shake; but the Lord will be the hope of his people, and the strength of the children of Israel." There you see the two sides: the great judgment but also the hope of salvation for God's people.

b) Salvation

When Jesus returns it won't all be all judgment; there also will be salvation for His people.

(1) Luke 21:27-28—Jesus told His disciples that when people see "the Son of man coming in a cloud, with power and great glory," they will look up and lift up their heads, for their redemption will be drawing near.

(2) Romans 11:26-27—"All Israel shall be saved; as it is written, There shall come out of Zion the Deliverer, and shall turn away ungodliness from Jacob; for this is my covenant unto them, when I shall take away their sins." Christ is that Deliverer. He will remove sin and grant salvation.

(3) Jeremiah 31:3-4—Jeremiah talks about what's going to happen when the children of Israel are delivered in the last days: "The Lord hath appeared of old unto me, saying, Yea, I have loved thee with an everlasting love; therefore with lovingkindness have I drawn thee. Again I will build thee, and thou shalt be built, O virgin of Israel;

24

thou shalt again be adorned with thy timbrels, and shalt go forth in the dances of those who make merry."

Review

I. THE HUMAN CONQUEROR (vv. 1-8)

A. The Purging by God (vv. 1-7; see pp. 11-17)

B. The Protection by God (v. 8; see pp. 17-18)

After prophesying about Alexander the Great's campaign through the Middle East, Zechariah spans the centuries in verse 8 to the time of Christ's appearance. Christ is the Divine Conqueror who alone can protect Jerusalem from being overrun by her enemies. He will accomplish that divine protection when He returns to earth.

Lesson

II. THE DIVINE CONQUEROR (vv. 9-17)

A. His Character (v. 9)

"Rejoice greatly, O daughter of Zion; shout, O daughter of Jerusalem; behold thy King cometh unto thee; he is just, and having salvation; lowly, and riding upon an ass, and upon a colt, the foal of an ass."

The prophet says the coming of Israel's King is reason for the Jews to be happy. That's because He will bring judgment to their enemies and salvation for them. But this conqueror is different from Alexander; He is introduced as riding on a donkey, unlike Alexander, who is known to have ridden a white charger. Against the background of the invincible army of Alexander comes One who doesn't inspire fear but praise and peace. This is not a foreign tyrant but Israel's own King. He is not cruel and oppressive but just and merciful. Rather than an appearance of power,

He appears poor and meek. Zechariah says His coming is something to get ecstatic about. Let's examine the four elements to His character that we see here.

1. He is King

   This monarch is Israel's King and Redeemer, the promised seed of David, known as the Messiah. Isaiah spoke of Him when he said, "Unto us a child is born, unto us a son is given, and the government shall be upon his shoulder" (Isa. 9:6). His kingship was announced after His birth by the wise men (Matt. 2:2) and at His death by the sign placed on His cross, which read, "Jesus, of Nazareth, the King of the Jews" (John 19:19). When Jesus returns, He will take control of the world that Satan has usurped.

2. He is just

   The divine King is righteous in character, and He deals justly. No more will anyone be denied justice. Won't it be great to have a world where all decisions are made by One who is absolutely righteous and just?

3. He is Savior

   The divine King comes to save men from their sins. When Jesus was born, an angel said of Him, "Thou shalt call his name Jesus; for he shall save his people from their sins" (Matt. 1:21). We remember His saving work in the Lord's Table, which acknowledges our need for a Savior. Alexander was not a savior—let alone a righteous man. He was an insignificant monarch compared to Christ.

4. He is meek

   a) The general fulfillment of Christ's lowliness

   Christ's lowly, humble nature is quite different from that of Alexander. The Hebrew word translated "lowly" refers to those who are afflicted with suffering. It was also used in an economic sense to speak of someone with no money. When He was crucified, the soldiers cast lots for His undergarment, which was one of His few possessions (John 19:23-24). The Lord told would-be disciples, "The foxes have holes, and the birds of the air have nests, but the Son of man hath not where to lay his head" (Matt. 8:20). His home was the Mount of Olives, where He often went to commune with His Father. He may have stayed in the homes of disciples such as Mary, Martha, and Lazarus.

b) The specific fulfillment of Zechariah's prophecy

The portrait of the Messiah riding upon a donkey in Zechariah 9:9 illustrates His meekness. Early in Israel's history, it was respectable to ride a donkey, but by Solomon's time (c. 1000 B.C.) it was not. Jeremiah (c. 625 B.C.) acknowledges that kings and princes rode on horses: "Then shall there enter into the gates of this city kings and princes sitting on the throne of David, riding in chariots and on horses" (17:25).

For the mighty Messiah to arrive on a donkey's colt would have seemed incongruous in the time of Christ. Nevertheless, that's what Jesus did, thus fulfilling Zechariah 9:9 (Matt. 21:1-5).

(1) The request of the Prince

Matthew 21 says, "When they drew near unto Jerusalem, and were come to Bethphage, unto the Mount of Olives, then sent Jesus two disciples, saying unto them, Go into the village opposite you, and straightway ye shall find an ass tied, and a colt with her; loose them, and bring them unto me. And if any man say anything unto you, ye shall say, The Lord hath need of them; and straightway he will send them" (vv. 1-3). Jesus, the Son of God, knew where He could find a donkey that He would be allowed to ride.

(2) The reaffirmation of the prophecy

Matthew points out that "all this was done, that it might be fulfilled which was spoken by the proph-

27

et, saying, Tell ye the daughter of Zion, behold, thy King cometh unto thee, meek, and sitting upon an ass, and a colt, the foal of an ass" (vv. 4-5). Zechariah's prophecy was fulfilled exactly as it had been given.

(3) The reception of the people

As Jesus approached Jerusalem by donkey the week prior to His crucifixion, "a very great multitude spread their garments in the way; others cut down branches from the trees, and spread them in the way. And the multitudes that went before, and that followed, cried, saying, Hosanna to the Son of David! Blessed is he that cometh in the name of the Lord! Hosanna in the highest!" (vv. 8-9). Jesus fulfilled the prophecy of the messianic King humbly riding on a donkey.

B. His Conquest (vv. 10-15)

At verse 10 we span the centuries again as we move from the first coming of Christ to His second coming. You might wonder why the Old Testament prophets jumped from one century to another in a single context. That's because they didn't know about the church age. It was a mystery—something hidden in the Old Testament but revealed in the New (cf. Eph. 3:3-6). They assumed the King would come and establish His kingdom at the same time. The church is a historical parenthesis until God begins dealing with Israel again during the Tribulation. Therefore it is not unusual to see two-thousand-year gaps between verses.

1. The reign of peace (v. 10)

"I will cut off the chariot from Ephraim, and the horse from Jerusalem, and the battle bow shall be cut off; and he shall speak peace unto the nations; and his dominion shall be from sea even to sea, and from the river even to the ends of the earth."

Zechariah moves from the deep humiliation and affliction of the Messiah at His first coming to the glory and exaltation of His second coming. The chariot mentioned here is a battle chariot, and the horse is an instrument of war. God is saying His Messiah will bring an end to war. He will remove the chariots, horses, and weapons from Israel because they won't have to fight anymore. Zechariah says the Messiah "shall speak peace unto the nations," which is the gist of Psalm 72, a messianic psalm. "From sea even to sea" means His rule will extend throughout the world. The river referred to here is the Euphrates, which was the eastern border of the land given originally to Abraham. This is a picture of God's wonderful redemption of Israel, when His Messiah will usher in a worldwide reign of peace.

2. The ratification of the promise (v. 11*a*)

"As for thee also, by the blood of thy covenant I have sent forth thy prisoners."

"I have sent forth" is in the perfect tense in the Hebrew text, conveying the idea that what is spoken of is as good as done. "The blood of thy covenant" refers to the covenant God made with Abraham in Genesis 15:1-6. He had promised to make a great nation of him and to bless that nation. He confirmed that promise with the sacrifice of a goat, ram, heifer, pigeon, and turtledove (v. 9). After Abraham cut the larger animals in half and placed the halves in two rows, God put him to sleep and ratified the covenant Himself as "a smoking furnace, and a burning lamp that passed between those pieces" (v. 17). In the culture of Abraham's day, covenants or contracts were made by two parties walking between the halves of an animal. God used the same practice but left Abraham out of the covenant-making process, making a unilateral covenant with Himself. Symbolized by fire and smoke, God passed alone through the animals Abraham had sacrificed and vowed to bless the patriarch's nation. That act made His promise unconditional, because God could never break a promise He made with Himself.

"The blood of thy covenant" may also refer to the bloodshed in the Mosaic covenant, and certainly it refers to the covenant that is ultimately fulfilled in the blood of Jesus Christ. Because of the covenants that God had already sealed and would be sealing with blood, God was promising through Zechariah that He would never violate His promise.

Amillennialists (those who believe the church has permanently replaced Israel) say that the Israelites aren't worthy to be redeemed because they forfeited their right to be the channel of God's blessing by their unfaithfulness. But God didn't say, "Israel, I'm going to bring you back because you're so wonderful," or, "because I feel sorry for you." Rather, He said, "I'm going to bring you back because I made a promise with Myself, and I sealed that promise in blood."

3. The release of the prisoners (v. 11b)

"I have sent forth thy prisoners out of the pit in which is no water."

A pit was a common place to put people you wanted to get rid of. Joseph's fate at the hands of his brothers is an example of how an individual might be left in a pit to die (Gen. 37:24). The pits were often empty cisterns that had been dug to store water. A pit without water was a dry well. God was saying that Israel had been in the dry well of captivity, suffering, and despair long enough. And because of His vow to Israel, they were as good as out. Zechariah's message would have been a great encouragement to the Jewish people, knowing that when the King came, Israel would be freed from the pit of trouble to experience the reign of the Prince of Peace.

4. The resource of the prisoners (v. 12)

"Turn to the stronghold, ye prisoners of hope; even today do I declare that I will render double unto thee."

God is saying, "Turn to Me in trust. All I have promised is going to come to pass. And when you get out, everything that's ever been withheld from you will be given back in double measure. After all, you've experienced double anxiety and suffering." Isaiah 61:7 offers a similar promise: "For your shame ye shall have double, and for confusion, they shall rejoice in their portion; there-

fore, in their land they shall possess a double portion."
God promises to deliver Israel from war and conflict and
give her peace and abundant blessing.

5. The rebellion of the people (v. 13)

"When I have bent Judah for me, filled the bow with
Ephraim, and raised up thy sons, O Zion, against thy
sons, O Greece, and made thee like the sword of a
mighty man."

Here's another historical pledge so that Israel wouldn't
lose its perspective of God's ultimate plan. The Lord
says, "Just to let you know I'm on your side and that
you need not doubt Me, even after Alexander, I'll give
you another victory to show that I will protect Israel."
Judah and Israel (Ephraim) are pictured as a bow and arrow that God promises to use as weapons against
Greece. There was only one time in history when God
used Israel to defeat Greece. It was during the intertes-
tamental period, the approximately four-hundred-year
period between the Old and New Testaments. That was
when Israel experienced the domination of Greece.
Only once did Israel ever break that domination—under
the leadership of the Maccabees, a prominent Jewish
family. Judas Maccabeus and his sons started a rebellion
against the yoke of Greece because of Antiochus Epiphanes, the despotic ruler who had desecrated the Temple. They led their people to fight against Greece and
prevailed.

6. The rebellion as a preview (v. 14)

"The Lord shall be seen over them, and his arrow shall
go forth like the lightning; and the Lord God shall blow
the trumpet, and go with whirlwinds of the south."

In the Middle East, violent storms come off the desert in
the south without warning. They illustrate the quick
and devastating manner in which God would use Israel
against Greece. The Maccabean rebellion lasted from
175 to 163 B.C. To them it was a holy war in which God
was their captain, calling them to battle with the sound
of His trumpet. But that war was only a preview of the

31

final victory, when Christ returns to deliver Israel during the Tribulation.

Commentator David Baron said, "Zion and Greece, as has been well observed by another writer, are in this prophecy of Zechariah opposed to one another as the city of God and the city of the world. . . . and the defeat of Antiochus Epiphanes and his successors at the hands of comparative handfuls of despised Jews, to which this passage may primarily refer, foreshadows the final conflict with world-power and the judgments to be inflicted on the confederated armies who shall be gathered against Jerusalem, not only directly by the hand of God, but also by the hand of Israel, who shall then be made strong in Jehovah, so that 'the feeble among them shall in that day be as David, and the house of David shall be as God, as the Angel of Jehovah before them' " (*The Visions & Prophecies of Zechariah* [Grand Rapids: Kregel, 1972], p. 327). What we see here in Zechariah is another historical picture of God's ultimate victory over the nations with Israel as His instrument.

7. The resource of protection (v. 15*a*)

"The Lord of hosts shall defend them; and they shall devour, and subdue the sling-stones."

That which is translated "the Lord of hosts" is literally "the Lord of armies" in the Hebrew text. The Lord will defend Israel and enable them to devour their enemy as a lion devours its prey. Devouring speaks of consuming something and acquiring its strengths. When you eat, your body assimilates the nutritional value of the food and transforms it into energy. Similarly, to conquer a certain country is to take all its resources and strengths and make them your own. This prophecy predicted Israel's taking the strength of its enemies and increasing its own strength.

"Sling-stones" were stones shot at enemies and their fortifications with slingshots and catapults. Zechariah prophesied that such weapons would not deter Israel's advance against the enemy. The stones would fall to the ground and be trodden over by Israel.

32

8. The rejoicing of the people (v. 15b)

"They shall drink, and make a noise as through wine; and they shall be filled like bowls, and like the corners of the altar."

The first part refers to the boisterous shouting that is typical of people who drink too much. However, Israel's excitement will be the rejoicing of their victory celebration.

The bowls referred to here are those used to catch the blood of animal sacrifices offered upon the altar. The priests would take the blood that had been collected and sprinkle it on the corners and sides of the altar. That is symbolic of the bloodshed of Israel's godless enemies. The ultimate battle in view here is Armageddon, where the armies of the world amass themselves against Israel during the Tribulation. It is a terrible picture of bloodshed so profuse that Israel will feel like the bowls upon the altar. Revelation 14:20 says that the blood will be up to the level of horses' bridles for two hundred miles.

C. His Care (vv. 16-17)

1. The redemption of the remnant (v. 16)

"The Lord, their God, shall save them in that day as the flock of his people; for they shall be like the stones of a crown, lifted up as an ensign upon his land."

In this verse the Messiah is seen as a Shepherd who is saving His flock. Zechariah 13:1 pictures that as a time of spiritual cleansing: "In that day there shall be a fountain opened to the house of David and to the inhabitants of Jerusalem for sin and for uncleanness." It may be that because the Messiah is a Shepherd to His people, the theme song of the kingdom He establishes will be Psalm 23, which begins, "The Lord is my shepherd; I shall not want."

The redeemed are referred to as jewels in the Messiah's crown, lifted up for all to see. Of a similar godly remnant Malachi 3:17 says, "They shall be mine, saith the

33

Lord of hosts, in that day when I make up my jewels."
This picture foretells a glorious future for Israel.

2. The response of the redeemed (v. 17)

"For how great is his goodness, and how great is his beauty! Grain shall make the young men cheerful, and new wine, the maids."

The only reasonable response is one of praise. The grain and the wine are symbols of the abundance of the kingdom. There will be prosperity and joy unlike the world has ever conceived.

Conclusion

The King is coming. He is none other than the Lord Jesus Christ, who came once in humility, riding upon the foal of a donkey, but will return in honor as the mighty Judge of the nations and Savior of His people. He came in poverty and shame but will return triumphant. Zechariah comforted Israel, telling them that some day their troubles would be over and salvation would come to them as they reign with their King. And in case they doubted that, he gave them the examples of how God used Alexander the Great and the Maccabees to preserve Israel as proof that He will fulfill the promises of His kingdom.

Peter said that Christ's future return ought to have a practical impact on our lives: "Seeing, then, that all these things shall be dissolved, what manner of persons ought ye to be in all holy living and godliness?" (2 Pet. 3:11). We ought to examine our hearts to determine the nature of our relationship to Christ. We also ought to go to those around us and call them to be a part of the kingdom. The apostle Paul said we should be "giving thanks unto the Father, who hath made us fit to be partakers of the inheritance of the saints in light; who hath delivered us from the power of darkness, and hath translated us into the kingdom of his dear Son; in whom we have redemption through his blood, even the forgiveness of sins" (Col. 1:12-14). The only reason you and I will ever enter that kingdom is that we love Jesus Christ. Although Zechariah was focusing on the restoration of Israel at that point, we become the spiritual seed of Abraham when we believe in Christ (Gal. 3:7-9). We need to thank Him for that privilege.

Focusing on the Facts

1. What is one reason for the injustice, conflict, and chaos in the world? When will those problems be resolved (see p. 22)?
2. Identify the positive and negative elements of Christ's return. How were they symbolically experienced in a vision by the apostle John (see pp. 22-23)?
3. Why is God's judgment difficult to comprehend (see p. 23)?
4. According to Jeremiah 31:3-4, why does God say He will restore Israel (see pp. 24-25)?
5. In Zechariah 9:9, how does the divine conqueror come to His people (see p. 25)?
6. Identify the divine conqueror of Zechariah 9, and describe His character (v. 9; see pp. 25-26).
7. How was the Messiah's meekness expressed in general and specific terms (v. 9; see pp. 26-27)?
8. Why do some Old Testament prophecies jump from one century to another in a single context (see p. 28)?
9. How is the Messiah's reign over His earthly kingdom described in verse 10 (see pp. 28-29)?
10. What did God point to as verification that He would fulfill His promise to His people (see p. 29)?
11. How were covenants, or contracts, often made in the ancient Middle East? How and why did God alter that tradition in His covenant with Abraham (see p. 29)?
12. What encouragement does God offer His people in verses 11-12 (see pp. 30-31)?
13. What historical insight does God use to encourage Israel in verse 13 (see p. 31)?
14. Of what was the Maccabean rebellion a preview (see pp. 31-32)?
15. Who will protect Israel and enable them to subdue their enemies (see p. 32)?
16. Why is Israel likened to the sacrificial bowls and altar (v. 15; see p. 33)?
17. What is Zechariah's response in verse 17 to the salvation promised in verse 16 (see p. 34)?
18. Although He first came in poverty and shame, how will Christ return (see p. 34)?

Pondering the Principles

1. It's not difficult to recognize that there are many problems in the world. Unbelievers cite the evidence of injustice, conflict, pain, and tragedy as proof that there is no God. Rather than blaming God for sin, as Adam did (Gen. 3:12), we need to acknowledge that man himself is the problem (vv. 17-19). When you next have the opportunity to answer the question, "What is this world coming to?" be sure to explain that the King of kings and Lord of lords is coming to set things right. Express your confident hope in a future where Christ actively reigns. Memorize 1 Peter 1:3-4: "Blessed be the God and Father of our Lord Jesus Christ, who according to His great mercy has caused us to be born again to a living hope through the resurrection of Jesus Christ from the dead, to obtain an inheritance which is imperishable and undefiled and will not fade away, reserved in heaven for you" (NASB*). Pray for an opportunity to tell others about our "living hope."

2. Are you letting the promise of Christ's return affect your life in the present? If we know that God's plan is to eliminate evil and bring His children into a perfect kingdom, we should make sure our lives are reflecting that holy purpose. Why would we pursue sin if it is the object of His hatred? That is the issue Peter asks his readers to think through in 2 Peter 3:10-14. Meditate upon that passage, and determine whether your life-style is coinciding with God's plan.

*New American Standard Bible.

3

The Redemption of Israel

Outline

Introduction

Lesson
  I. A Divine Redeemer (v. 4)
     A. His Identity Implied
     B. His Impact Illustrated
        1. As a cornerstone
        2. As a nail
        3. As a battle bow
 II. A Divine Rain (v. 1)
     A. Literal Rain
     B. Spiritual Blessing
III. A Divine Recompense (vv. 2-3)
     A. The Problem (v. 2)
        1. The indictment of the false shepherds
        2. The identity of the future Shepherd
     B. The Punishment (v. 3)
 IV. A Divine Restoration (vv. 5-7a)
  V. A Divine Rejoicing (v. 7b)
 VI. A Divine Regathering (vv. 8-11)
     A. The Call to the Redeemed (v. 8)
     B. The Collection of the Remnant (vv. 9-10)
        1. Isaiah 54:1-2
        2. Isaiah 49:20-22
     C. The Clearing of Roadblocks (v. 11)
VII. A Divine Renovation (v. 12)

Introduction

Romans 11:1 asks a question that theologians and students of the Bible still discuss today: "Hath God cast away his people?" Paul answers it succinctly in the next verse: "God hath not cast away his people whom he foreknew." Romans 11 deals with the fulfillment of God's promises to Israel and declares His faithfulness in not setting them aside. After explaining God's plan for Israel, Paul ends the chapter by saying, "All Israel shall be saved; as it is written, There shall come out of Zion the Deliverer, and shall turn away ungodliness from Jacob; for this is my covenant unto them, when I shall take away their sins. . . . For the gifts and callings of God are without repentance" (vv. 26-29; cf. Isa. 59:20-21). Has God forgotten about His promises to Israel? No. Chapter 11 emphatically states that He will save them.

One of the most wonderful things we can tell Jewish people is that there's a great future ahead for Israel—God is going to redeem the nation. America's Christian heritage is one of the reasons she has been such a great friend to Israel. The Israelis know that many Americans, especially evangelical Christians, believe in the restoration of Israel.

Isaiah 59:20-21, which Paul quoted in Romans 11, says, "The Redeemer shall come to Zion, and unto those who turn from transgression in Jacob, saith the Lord. As for me, this is my covenant with them, saith the Lord: My Spirit that is upon thee, and my words which I have put in thy mouth, shall not depart out of thy mouth, nor out of the mouth of thy seed, nor out of the mouth of thy seed's seed, saith the Lord, from henceforth and forever." God says there is a forever planned for Israel that culminates when the Redeemer returns to Israel. He will turn them away from their ungodliness and forgive their sins. But what is involved in their redemption, and what are the benefits of that salvation? The answer to those questions form the theme of Zechariah 10.

Lesson

I. A DIVINE REDEEMER (v. 4)

"Out of him came forth the corner, out of him the nail, out of him the battle bow, out of him every oppressor together."

A. His Identity Implied

Zechariah reminds the people that the Messiah is coming, and he identifies Him in this verse. This verse is one of the richest messianic prophecies in the Old Testament. Zechariah, a post-exilic (latter) prophet picks up three illustrations from pre-exilic (former) prophets regarding the Messiah. He refers to Him as a cornerstone, a nail, and a battle bow. Those three terms give us tremendous insight into the Messiah.

The phrase "out of him" refers back to the house of Judah in verse 3. The Deliverer who came from the house of Judah is the Lord Jesus Christ. Scripture not only identifies Him as the lion of the tribe of Judah (Rev. 5:5; cf. Gen. 49:10) but also records His being born at the messianic birthplace of Bethlehem (Matt. 2:1). Micah 5:2 says, "Thou, Bethlehem Ephrathah, though thou be little among the thousands of Judah, yet out of thee shall he come forth unto me that is to be ruler in Israel, whose goings forth have been from of old, from everlasting."

B. His Impact Illustrated

1. As a cornerstone

Zechariah states that "out of him came forth the corner," which refers to a cornerstone. That messianic title was used by the former prophets and the New Testament authors several times.

a) Isaiah 28:16—"Thus saith the Lord God, Behold I lay in Zion for a foundation a stone, a tested stone, a precious cornerstone, a sure foundation; he that believeth shall not make haste." The apostle Peter identifies that stone as Jesus Christ (1 Pet. 2:5-7).

b) Romans 9:32-33—Paul here repeats what Isaiah said: "[Israel] stumbled at that stumbling stone; as it is written, Behold, I lay in Zion a stumbling stone and a rock of offense; and whosoever believeth on him shall not be ashamed." Paul was referring to the rejection of Jesus Christ by Israel, which was seeking righteousness by works.

c) 1 Corinthians 1:23—Paul said, "We preach Christ crucified, unto the Jews a stumbling block."

d) Ephesians 2:20—The church is "built upon the foundation of the apostles and prophets, Jesus Christ himself being the chief cornerstone." Sometimes He's referred to as a stone of stumbling and sometimes as a cornerstone.

e) 1 Peter 2:6-8—Here Peter combined both metaphors of a cornerstone and stumbling stone and applied them to Christ.

f) Daniel 2:34—Daniel referred to the Messiah as a stone "cut out without hands" coming in judgment to destroy the Gentile world powers. Jesus alludes to that crushing aspect of the messianic stone in Matthew 21:44.

Although the Messiah is pictured as a stone of judgment, that is not the emphasis in Zechariah. As a cornerstone gives stability to its adjoining walls and is the principal foundation of a building, so Christ is the foundation upon which His kingdom rests. He is the One who will come and give stability to Israel.

Commentator David Baron said, "The great God, the Divine Architect of the universe, has purposed within Himself from all eternity to raise out of frail, imperfect, human materials a glorious Temple for His own eternal habitation through the Spirit, which, when completed, shall show forth, even more than the material temple of the universe, to principalities and powers the infinite power and manifold wisdom of God; and in order to insure its eternal safety He has bestowed great care on the foundation. He Himself has laid it. . . . And the 'tried' and 'precious' corner-stone which He laid as the basis of this mystical structure is His own Son, who is 'perfected for evermore,' against whom even the gates of hell shall not prevail" (*The Visions & Prophecies of Zechariah* [Grand Rapids: Kregel, 1972], p. 348). When God sets Christ as the cornerstone, the foundation stands sure. History has shown that His church has weathered the storms of satanic and human opposition.

Just as a cornerstone supports two walls, so Christ holds up the two walls that constitute His redeemed people—the church and Israel. Although there used to be a wall between Jew and Gentile, there is now a common cornerstone. Some day when Israel enters her earthly kingdom, the Gentiles who are saved will enter it with her. By the time we enter the eternal state, there probably won't be any way to tell us apart. So all those who know and love the Lord Jesus Christ and who are of Jewish descent will fit into either wall.

2. As a nail

The Hebrew word translated "nail" refers to two kinds of nails. One is a tent stake. The other is a nail or peg that was driven into the center pole of the tent or built into the wall of a dwelling. Utensils and valuables were hung on it. Often the wealth of a family would be hung on that peg for the admiration of all who came in. I believe Zechariah had in mind this latter idea, implying that God is going to make Christ the nail in the midst of His kingdom, for all the glory of the kingdom will hang on Him. Zechariah 6:13 says that the Messiah "shall build the temple of the Lord; and he shall bear the glory." Christ will bear the glory of His millennial kingdom's splendor within the Temple He builds.

41

Isaiah 22 supports the idea of a such a peg's referring to Christ. The close historical fulfillment of Isaiah's messianic prophecy was Eliakim, the master of King Hezekiah's household. Speaking of him as a prototype of the Messiah, God says, "I will fasten him like a nail in a sure place; and he shall be for a glorious throne to his father's house. And they shall hang upon him all the glory of his father's house, the offspring and the issue, all vessels of small quantity, from the vessels of cups, even to the vessels of flagons" (vv. 23-24).

3. As a battle bow

Zechariah also refers to the messianic Redeemer as "the battle bow." Zechariah 9:13 says, "I have bent Judah for me, filled the bow with Ephraim, and raised up thy sons, O Zion, against thy sons, O Greece, and made thee like the sword of a mighty man." There God is pictured as if He were an archer using His people as a bow and arrow against the Greek invader, Antiochus Epiphanes. In chapter 10 the Messiah is portrayed as the battle bow itself. He is a conqueror without equal who will come and destroy the enemy. That's the picture we have of Christ in Revelation 19:11-16. Zechariah 9:13 tells us that the Messiah will put out every oppressor of Israel.

II. A DIVINE RAIN (v. 1)

"Ask of the Lord rain in the time of the latter rain; so the Lord shall make bright clouds, and give them showers of rain, to every one grass in the field."

Zechariah said in the previous verse that God is going to bring great harvests of grain and grapes in the millennial kingdom. In this verse he encourages the Jewish people to request the Lord's blessings of His kingdom.

A. Literal Rain

"Showers of rain" doesn't refer to a violent, destructive rain but an ample productive rain. I believe Zechariah is referring in part to literal rain. In the millennial kingdom God is going to cause rain to allow the crops of that dry part of the world to flourish. I've been out on the desert outside of Jerusalem to the east, and there's nothing significant growing out there now.

Isaiah 35 gives us a picture of how the Lord will shower His earthly kingdom: "The wilderness and the solitary place shall be glad for them; and the desert shall rejoice, and blossom like the rose. It shall blossom abundantly, and rejoice even with joy and singing; the glory of Lebanon shall be given unto it, the excellency of Carmel and Sharon. . . . In the wilderness shall waters break out, and streams in the desert. And the parched ground shall become a pool, and the thirsty land springs of water; in the habitation of jackals, where each lay, shall be grass with reeds and rushes" (vv. 1-2, 6-7). In the Millennium the inland desert is going to look like the lush green coastal areas of Israel. But for that to happen, there is going to have to be some divine rain.

B. Spiritual Blessing

Although the Bible promises a literal kingdom with literal rain and literal fields and crops, it also speaks of spiritual blessing outpoured on the people of God. The blossoming desert is an illustration of how God will bless the millennial kingdom.

Hosea declared, "Come, and let us return unto the Lord; for he hath torn, and he will heal us; he hath smitten, and he will bind us up. After two days will he revive us; in the third day he will raise us up, and we shall live in his sight. Then shall we know, if we follow on to know the Lord; his going forth is prepared as the morning; and he shall come unto us as the rain, as the latter and former rain unto the earth" (6:1-3). God's outpoured blessing is likened to the rain. That promise refers not only to the spring rain that comes in March and April that's so indispensable to the crops, but also to the rain of God's blessing.

III. A DIVINE RECOMPENSE (vv. 2-3)

A. The Problem (v. 2)

"The idols have spoken vanity, and the diviners have seen a lie, and have told false dreams; they comfort in vain; therefore, they went their way like a flock; they were troubled, because there was no shepherd."

This verse is a sad picture of Israel's spiritual life before the Babylonian captivity. Although the captivity cured the nation of its idolatry, it was the result of their idolatry in the first place. The people of Israel worshiped idols and followed diviners (occultic fortune tellers), who led them into error. The Hebrew word translated "idols" (*teraphim*) refers primarily to household idols. Pagan worshipers did not confine their worship to temples but used household idols of their gods, which often became channels of demonism.

Idolatry was not unusual in Israel. Genesis 31:19, 1 Samuel 15:23, and 2 Kings 23:24 record it as an ever-increasing problem in Israel's history, even though it was absolutely forbidden by God. The wicked and useless guidance of demon-inspired idolatry, along with the deception and false comfort of the diviners, left Israel like sheep without a shepherd.

1. The indictment of the false shepherds

Ezekiel prophesied about that tragedy: "My sheep wandered through all the mountains, and upon every high hill; yea, my flock was scattered upon all the face of the earth, and none did search or seek after them. Therefore, ye shepherds, hear the word of the Lord. As I live, saith the Lord God, surely, because my flock became a prey, and my flock became food to every beast of the field, because there was no shepherd, neither did my shepherds search for my flock, but the shepherds fed themselves, and fed not my flock, Therefore, O ye shepherds, hear the word of the Lord. Thus saith the Lord God: Behold, I am against the shepherds, and I will require my flock at their hand, and cause them to cease from feeding the flock, neither shall the shepherds feed themselves any more; for I will deliver my flock from their mouth, that they may not be food for them" (Ezek. 34:6-10). God condemns the religious leaders of Israel for having selfishly used His people to benefit themselves. Although the people provided food for them through their offerings, the religious leaders had failed to spiritually nourish the flock. God was angered because they had left His people to wander about by themselves without a shepherd.

2. The identity of the future Shepherd

In Ezekiel 34 God says, "Therefore will I save my flock. . . . I will set up one shepherd over them, and he shall feed them, even my servant, David; he shall feed them, and he shall be their shepherd. And I, the Lord, will be their God . . . I, the Lord, have spoken it" (vv. 22-24). God will give His people a faithful Shepherd, the Messiah, who was symbolized by David because of God's promise to him (2 Sam. 7:4-17).

B. The Punishment (v. 3)

"Mine anger was kindled against the shepherds, and I punished the goats; for the Lord of hosts hath visited his flock, the house of Judah, and hath made them as his majestic horse in the battle."

The Hebrew term translated "goats" (lit., "he-goats") is used in the Old Testament to refer to leaders or chiefs. False leaders—just as they did in the past—will draw God's people into occultic practices and idolatry.

In the future I believe Israel is going to return to the worship of idols and to occultic practices, as verse 2 implies. Daniel 9:27 tells us that during the Tribulation Israel will make a pact with the Antichrist, who will set up an image to himself in the Jerusalem Temple and require everyone to bow to it. When the doors of hell open and the demons are released, there will be demonic activity in the world like never before (Rev. 9:1-21). Israel will become engulfed in occultic idolatry. But in the end, God will look with mercy on His people who have been victimized by false leaders.

God will allow His people to experience an incredible delusion. But after He lets the satanic forces of evil run their limit, He will destroy them. Isaiah 66:4 says, "I also will choose their delusions, and will bring their fears upon them, because when I called, none did answer; when I spoke, they did not hear; but they did evil before mine eyes, and chose that in which I delighted not." Yet in His wonderful grace, the divine Redeemer will come in the midst of that delusion as a true shepherd and use the nation of Israel to conquer His foes.

Zechariah 10:3 tells us essentially the same thing that we find later in 12:1-9 and 14:1-8, as well as the apocalyptic prophecies of Isaiah, Ezekiel, and John—that Christ is going to come in judgment using the nation of Israel as His war horse. Zechariah 12:9 says, "It shall come to pass, in that day, that I will seek to destroy all the nations that come against Jerusalem."

IV. A DIVINE RESTORATION (vv. 5-7a)

"They shall be like mighty men, who tread down their enemies in the mire of the streets in the battle; and they shall fight, because the Lord is with them, and the riders on horses shall be confounded. And I will strengthen the house of Judah, and I will save the house of Joseph [Israel], and I will bring them again to place them [in their land]; for I have mercy upon them, and they shall be as though I had not cast them off; for I am the Lord, their God, and will hear them. And they of Ephraim shall be like a mighty man."

A tremendous restoration is going to come to the nation of Israel, which will be transformed into a powerful army by God. If you study Israel's history in Scripture, you will discover that the only time the nation ever won a battle was when the Lord was in it. Such will be the case in the end times. Because the Lord will be with them, they will confound their enemies ("the riders on horses"). In their confusion, the defeated nations will be ashamed of their inability to withstand Israel. They will be in a state of shock when the King of kings joins with His mighty people from Israel to win the great and final battle before the earthly kingdom is established.

"The house of Judah" refers to the southern kingdom of Israel and "the house of Joseph" to the northern. God is going to restore the whole nation by bringing them back to the land (cf. Jer. 32:37). That's a great message to the Jewish people, who have been wandering throughout the world for so many centuries.

At the restoration of Israel, it will be as though God had never set them aside. This clear prophecy of Israel having a place in the kingdom, given here in verses 5-7 and in many other places, makes its difficult to see how people could believe that God will never restore Israel. It's God's plan to strengthen "they of Ephraim" (another name for Israel) and restore them to the place of blessing. They'll be given the position intended for them from the beginning.

You might wonder why God is going to do this. It is simply because He is "the Lord, their God." The Hebrew equivalent of the title translated "Lord" here identifies His covenant-keeping nature. He performs that which He promises. No longer will He consider them "Lo-ruhamah" (Hosea 1:6, "unpitied") or "Lo-ammi" (Hosea 1:9, "not my people"), names symbolic of the periods of Israel's history when they were separated from God. Israel will again become God's people who acknowledge Him as their God.

V. A DIVINE REJOICING (v. 7b)

"Their heart shall rejoice as through wine; yea, their children shall see it, and be glad; their heart shall rejoice in the Lord."

Naturally when the divine Redeemer comes and brings His judgment upon the wicked and His blessing upon His people, there will be great joy. The joy of the restored nation of Israel is likened to those who have had a little too much to drink. Everyone's going to be rejoicing in the Lord, including the children.

Isaiah predicted joy that would be a great contrast to the sorrow Israel had experienced over the centuries: "Rejoice with Jerusalem, and be glad with her, all ye that love her; rejoice for joy with her, all ye that mourn for her, that ye may nurse, and be satisfied with the breasts of her consolations; that ye may drink deeply, and be delighted with the abundance of her glory. For thus saith the Lord: Behold, I will extend peace to her like a river, and the glory of the nations like a flowing stream; then shall ye be nursed, ye shall be borne upon her sides, and be dandled upon her knees. As one whom his mother comforteth, so will I comfort you, and ye shall be comforted in Jerusalem. And when ye see this, your heart shall rejoice, and your bones shall flourish like an herb; and the hand of the Lord shall be known toward his servants" (Isa. 66:10-14). Jerusalem is going to be like a nursing mother who comforts her children. The rest of the world will experience the joy of Jerusalem, as a child shares in the joy of his mother when she bounces him on her knee.

VI. A DIVINE REGATHERING (vv. 8-11)

A. The Call to the Redeemed (v. 8)

"I will hiss [whistle] for them, and gather them; for I have redeemed them, and they shall increase as they have increased."

When the divine Redeemer returns, He will whistle for His people and regather them (cf. Isa. 5:26). They will multiply as they did in Egypt (Ex. 1:8-22). Prior to their redemption before the millennial kingdom, the people of Israel are going to continue to flourish into a mighty nation, in spite of any persecution they may encounter.

Those who become saved during the Tribulation and survive it will enter into the earthly millennial kingdom in physical, nonglorified bodies. (All other believers will already have received physical, glorified bodies.) They will have children and will live a long time. In fact, if someone dies at a hundred, it will be considered a short life span (Isa. 65:20). The earth will be filled with children. Zechariah 2:4 says, "Jerusalem shall be inhabited like towns without walls for the multitude of men and cattle in it."

B. The Collection of the Remnant (vv. 9-10)

"I will sow them among the peoples; and they shall remember me in far countries, and they shall live with their children, and turn again. I will bring them again also out of the land of Egypt, and gather them out of Assyria; and I will bring them into the land of Gilead and Lebanon, and place shall not be found for them."

Verse 9 backs up in history to when God sowed His people among the nations. That prophecy was fulfilled in A.D. 70, when the Jewish people were scattered all over the world. Egypt and Assyria are symbols of all the countries in which they have been scattered. Even within the larger territory promised to Israel in the covenants (symbolized by Gilead and Lebanon), there will not be enough room because of the multitude of Jewish people.

1. Isaiah 54:1-2—"Sing, O barren, thou who didst not bear; break forth into singing, and cry aloud, thou who didst not travail with child; for more are the children of the desolate than the children of the married wife, saith the Lord. Enlarge the place of thy tent, and let them stretch forth the curtains of thine habitations; spare not, lengthen thy cords, and strengthen thy stakes." Here Isaiah also prophesied about Israel's population explosion in the end times. He pictured their having to increase the size of their tents, using longer ropes and stakes that are more securely anchored.

2. Isaiah 49:20-22—"The children whom thou shalt have, after thou hast lost the other, shall say again in thine ears, The place is too narrow for me; give a place to me that I may dwell. Then shalt thou say in thine heart, Who hath begotten me these, seeing I have lost my children, and am desolate, a captive, and moving to and fro? And who hath brought up these? Behold, I was left alone; these, where had they been? Thus saith the Lord God: Behold, I will lift up mine hand to the nations, and set up my standard to the peoples; and they shall bring thy sons in their arms, and thy daughters shall be carried upon their shoulders." Israel will wonder where all her children came from, having assumed they were permanently lost in the Dispersion. God will even use the Gentile nations to bring the people of Israel back to their land, but when they get there they'll find there won't be enough room because of the multitudes regathering.

C. The Clearing of Roadblocks (v. 11)

"He shall pass through the sea with affliction, and shall smite the waves in the sea, and all the deeps of the river shall dry up; and the pride of Assyria shall be brought down, and the scepter of Egypt shall depart."

To gather all these people when He whistles for them, God's going to have to remove some obstacles. Passing through the sea is an allusion to the dividing of the Red Sea. In the context of the verse, "the deeps of the river" refers to the Nile, which will dry up in the manner of the Jordan River when Israel marched across it to enter the Promised Land. God will remove not only geographical obstacles as He regathers His people but also political ones. He will conquer the pride of a nation like Assyria and the dominance of a nation like Egypt to enable His people to return unhindered. Assyria and Egypt, the traditional enemies of Israel, symbolize any nation that would try to withhold God from fulfilling His will. God will overcome any obstacle to get His people back.

VII. A DIVINE RENOVATION (v. 12)

"I will strengthen them in the Lord; and they shall walk up and down in his name, saith the Lord."

God will bring about a total spiritual revival among His people. As those who "shall walk up and down in his name," the people of Israel will be the messengers of their Messiah in the millennial kingdom. What a glorious future there will be for Israel!

It's great to know where history's going, but it's even greater to be a part of it. We who know Christ will witness the transformation of the earth and experience the blessings of His kingdom.

Focusing on the Facts

1. What question does Paul answer in Romans 11 (see p. 38)?
2. What is one of the most wonderful things we can tell Jewish people about Israel (see p. 38)?
3. Where was the Messiah to come from? Who specifically fulfilled that prophecy? Support your answer with Scripture (vv. 3-4; see p. 39).
4. The Messiah was pictured as what kind of stones? Describe the significance of both (see pp. 39-41).
5. What do the analogies of a nail and a battle bow teach us about the Messiah (see pp. 41-42)?
6. Explain the nature of the rain that God will send in the Millennium (see pp. 42-43).
7. What was the result of Israel's idolatry, and what did that result have upon their idolatry (see p. 44)?
8. Why was Israel like sheep without a shepherd (see pp. 44-45)?
9. According to Ezekiel 34:8, what did Israel's shepherds fail to do? What will her future Shepherd do, according to verses 22-24 (see p. 45)?
10. What will false leaders do to God's people during the Tribulation? How will the Lord of hosts respond (see pp. 45-46)?
11. When were the only times Israel ever won its battles? What will enable the nation to win the final battle in the end times (vv. 5-6; see p. 46)?
12. Why will God restore the nation of Israel (see p. 47)?
13. What will be the response of those who experience God's blessing and victory over their enemies (v. 7b; see p. 47)?
14. In spite of persecution, what will happen to the people of Israel (v. 8; see p. 48)?
15. When did God sow His children "among the peoples" (v. 9)? Why will a place not be found for them when God regathers them (see p. 49)?
16. What kind of obstacles will God remove to get His people back into their land (see p. 50)?
17. How will God's people be strengthened in the Millennium? How will they serve the Messiah (v. 12; see p. 50)?

Pondering the Principles

1. Scripture identifies Christ as a cornerstone, a stumbling stone, and a judgment stone. How one perceives Christ determines the nature of one's relationship with Him. Have you acknowledged Christ as the cornerstone of God's kingdom and the sure foundation of your faith? As the parable of the builder implies, it is on the solid foundation of Christ and obedient faith in His commands that we must build our lives if we hope to withstand the storms of judgment (Matt. 7:24-27). Search your heart and discern whether you are truly trusting in Christ for your eternal life.

2. Pray for opportunities to reach Jewish people. Let them know that God is still in control and that He will be faithful in His promises to them. Review some of those promises covered in this chapter, and be ready to draw their attention to them. But point out that once a man dies, judgment is appointed, making it too late to make a decision for or against Christ, the Messiah (Heb. 9:27). Ask God to use this study of Christ's return to give you a sense of urgency in proclaiming the gospel and a renewed hope of heaven.

4

The Rejection of the True Shepherd

Outline

Introduction

Lesson
I. The Ravage of the Wailing Shepherds (vv. 1-3)
  A. The Land
  B. The Lions
  C. The Lament
    1. The human response
    2. The historical record
II. The Rejection of the True Shepherd (vv. 4-14)
  A. The Problem Expressed (vv. 4-6)
    1. The command about the condemned (v. 4)
    2. The condition of the condemned (v. 5)
      a) Oppressed from without (v. 5a)
      b) Ignored from within (v. 5b)
    3. The consequences of the condemned (v. 6)
      a) An absence of pity
      b) An absence of protection
  B. The Parable Enacted (vv. 7-14)
    1. The role of the shepherd (v. 7)
      a) His teaching (v. 7a)
      b) His tools (v. 7b)
    2. The rejection of the Shepherd (v. 8)
    3. The response of the Shepherd (vv. 9-14)
      a) Abandoning the unbelievers (v. 9)
      b) Breaking the covenant (v. 10)
      c) Confirming the word (v. 11)
      d) Being betrayed by the people (vv. 12-13)

(1) The determination of the price (v. 12)
(2) The distribution to the potter (v. 13)
  e) Forsaking the nation (v. 14)

Introduction

Zechariah 11 is a sad chapter. It stands out in stark contrast to chapters 9 and 10. It pictures the Messiah (whom we know to be Jesus Christ) as a Shepherd. That's a familiar concept to us because the Old Testament talks about God as a shepherd. In Psalm 23:1 David says, "The Lord is my shepherd." The prophet Isaiah said that the Lord God "shall feed his flock like a shepherd; he shall gather the lambs with his arm, and carry them in his bosom, and shall gently lead those that are with young" (Isa. 40:11). In John 10:11 Jesus says, "I am the good shepherd; the good shepherd giveth his life for the sheep." Such passages in the Old and New Testaments have endearing beauty to them. But Zechariah 11 is an exception to that rule. Zechariah presents an ugly picture of the rejection of the Messiah, the true Shepherd.

Through Zechariah God has promised salvation to Israel—a regathering and restoration in the land. But suddenly in chapter 11, the prophet of hope turns into a prophet of doom and judgment. He turns from the glories of the Messiah at His second coming to the national apostasy and rejection that occurred at His first coming, which is the main theme of the chapter. It helps us understand why the promises of chapters 9 and 10 didn't come to pass when Jesus came the first time.

Lesson

I. THE RAVAGE OF THE WAILING SHEPHERDS (vv. 1-3)

"Open thy doors, O Lebanon, that the fire may devour thy cedars. Wail, fir tree; for the cedar is fallen, because the mighty [glorious trees] are spoiled; wail, O ye oaks of Bashan; for the forest of the vintage is come down. There is a voice of the wailing of the shepherds; for their glory is spoiled; a voice of the roaring of young lions; for the pride of the Jordan is spoiled."

A. The Land

Those three verses are judgmental. They identify three different locations: Lebanon, Bashan, and Jordan. In the geography of Israel, that list begins in the north and descends to the south. It pictures judgment sweeping down like fire burning the vegetation in Lebanon and Bashan on down to the foliage around the Jordan Valley, where lions dwelt. The Holy Spirit used dramatic imagery to describe the ravaging of the whole land of Israel.

Zechariah was describing a fire of judgment that would consume the ungodly as a conflagration consumes trees. The trees symbolize portions of land. Lebanon was known for its cedars. The wood that was used to build Solomon's Temple was from the cedars of Lebanon (1 Kings 5).

Moving down from Lebanon, which is on the northern border of Israel, we come to the area of Bashan, which is east of the sea of Galilee. It was known for its oak trees. Descending further south we come to the Jordan Valley, in which runs the the Jordan River, extending from the Sea of Galilee to the Dead Sea. At one time there appears to have been dense, jungle-like foliage along both sides of the river.

I believe that the judgment God is speaking about here is an actual devastation. Although a literal fire that burns trees may not be involved, the devastation is not limited to spiritual judgment only. It includes the death of people as the land of Israel is being judged.

There's an inevitability to this judgment. In verse 1 Lebanon is told to open its doors, as if there's no sense in resisting. The fir and oak trees might as well wail, because if the mighty cedars, which are relatively inaccessible, go up in flames the other trees aren't going to be able to stand. When the high and the mighty are fallen, every lesser tree will be unable to escape. Some people have likened these trees to the leadership of Israel, assuming this is a spiritual judgment on the hierarchy of Israel, which includes the priests, elders, scribes, and runs all the way down to the common people.

B. The Lions

The "roaring of young lions" implies a repeat of the conditions after the captivity of the Northern Kingdom, when wild beasts began to multiply around the Jordan River (cf. 2 Kings 17:22-26; Jer. 49:19; 50:44). The lions dwelt in the thick foliage. The fierce young lions, which have voracious appetites, will roar when they see the coming devastation that will destroy their homes and food. Beyond that, the roaring of the lions and the wailing of the shepherds are poetic figures of the misery that will occur in the land when it's devastated. The idea of destruction is emphasized with a Hebrew verb meaning "to destroy," which is used three times in verses 1-3.

C. The Lament

1. The human response

Verse 3 says, "There is a voice of the wailing of the shepherds; for their glory is spoiled." These may be literal shepherds who are howling because the pastureland for their sheep has been devastated. Some say they may refer to the spiritual shepherds of Israel, and that would certainly fit with other scriptural references to leaders as shepherds. But regardless of their exact identity, they represent the human response as God's great judgment comes upon Israel.

2. The historical record

What destruction is Zechariah 11:1-3 referring to? At what point in Israel's history did this happen? The best and oldest interpretation (held by ancient rabbis and many modern scholars) is that it is referring to the destruction of Israel and Jerusalem in A.D. 70. Approximately forty years after Jesus was crucified, the Roman army destroyed Jerusalem, killing 1,100,000 Jews, according to Josephus (*Wars* 6.9.3). About sixty years later, the armies of the Roman emperor Hadrian destroyed 985 towns in the process of subduing the Bar Kokhba Revolt. These two devastations resulted in the scattering of the Jewish people throughout the world. But because of God's sovereignty the Jews have been preserved as a people, and it is only in this century that they have come back to their land.

It is difficult to comprehend the degree of devastation Israel experienced. The Romans might have destroyed an entire civilization had it not been preserved by God. The siege of Jerusalem led to such atrocities as some of the Jewish people eating their own children to avoid starvation.

II. THE REJECTION OF THE TRUE SHEPHERD (vv. 4-14)

I've studied many chapters in the Bible, but one of the most difficult I've ever studied is Zechariah 11. The chapter's poetic style is difficult to interpret; however, its main theme is clear in spite of our lack of understanding of some of the details. An important key to the chapter is understanding its style of prophetic utterance. In the Old Testament, prophets often prophesied by acting out a symbolic scene. Verbalizing God's revelation was not the only means of prophesying. For example, God instructed Isaiah to "take a great roll, and write in it with a man's pen concerning Maher-shalal-hash-baz [which means "make haste to the spoils"]" (Isa. 8:1). That was the name of Isaiah's second son, a symbolic demonstration of judgment upon Damascus and Samaria. God told Ezekiel to take a tile, draw the city of Jerusalem, and dramatically besiege it (Ezek. 4:1-2). Although onlookers may have believed the prophet had gone crazy, he was acting out a message from God to them. In Zechariah 11 God uses the prophet as an actor playing the part of a shepherd to illustrate the true Shepherd, Jesus Christ, and the rejection He encountered.

A. The Problem Expressed (vv. 4-6)

1. The command about the condemned (v. 4)

"Thus saith the Lord, my God: Feed the flock of the slaughter."

The Hebrew word translated "feed" encompasses the shepherd's responsibilities of leading and caring for his flock—along the lines of what Psalm 23 describes. In the case of Zechariah, feeding the flock would mean teaching the people. The prophet was a picture of the true Shepherd, who teaches His people the truth of God.

"The flock of the slaughter" is not an endearing phrase. God identified His covenant people as a flock intended for butchering. It's as if He were saying, "Since Israel will one day reject My Shepherd, they are designated as a flock for butchering. But I'm going to give them a chance: I'm going to feed them and see if they'll eat." He instructed Zechariah to go to the people of Israel who, in God's plan, were destined for a horrible devastation. Nevertheless He wanted to extend His grace by feeding them one more time. That's essentially what Jesus did. Forty years before the great butchering of Israel, God came and tried to feed the flock, but for the most part they refused to accept the Shepherd. Therefore they became a flock for slaughter.

2. The condition of the condemned (v. 5)

   a) Oppressed from without (v. 5a)

   "Whose possessors slay them, and hold themselves not guilty; and they that sell them say, Blessed be the Lord; for I am rich."

   Verses 5 and 6 form a brief parenthesis. Those who slay the flock are the foreign oppressors. Although it's true that God sovereignly handed Israel over to the nations for judgment, it's also true that the nations are responsible for their cruelty. God may have designed Israel for judgment, but that doesn't mean that when the nations superseded reasonable punishment they were without guilt.

   In Jeremiah 50:17-18 the Lord says, "Israel is a scattered sheep, the lions have driven him away; first the king of Assyria hath devoured him, and last this Nebuchadnezzar, king of Babylon, hath broken his bones. Therefore, thus saith the Lord of hosts, the God of Israel: Behold, I will punish the king of Babylon and his land, as I have punished the king of Assyria." God had ordained the kings of Assyria and Babylon to judge Israel, but that made them no less guilty for the sins of cruelty that they perpetrated. That may be a difficult concept for our finite minds to grasp, but we'll just have to leave it in the hands of a just God.

Zechariah says that the nations who slay Israel will "hold themselves not guilty." The Assyrians and Babylonians felt no remorse when they slaughtered Israel in the seventh and sixth centuries before Christ. Jeremiah 50:7 says, "All that found them have devoured them; and their adversaries said, We offend not, because they have sinned against the Lord." (Josephus wrote that Titus, the Roman general who led the siege, groaned when he saw valleys filled with the bodies of siege victims, "and spreading out his hands to heaven, called God to witness that this was not his doing" [*Wars* 5.12.4].) Those Gentile nations felt justified in inflicting punishment on God's sinful people. The Romans must have determined that what they were doing was a wonderful act of judgment. Zechariah tells us they mockingly thanked the Lord for the profit made from the spoils of the people they slaughtered. Josephus tells us that with the fall of Jerusalem in A.D. 70, the Romans sold tens of thousands of Jews into slavery (cf. *Wars* 6.9.3).

b) Ignored from within (v. 5*b*)

"Their own shepherds pity them not."

It was bad enough that the Gentile nations came in and slaughtered the people, but what made it worse was that Israel's leaders didn't do anything to defend their people or to avert their judgment. Israel's spiritual leaders had failed to teach the people the spiritual truths that could have led them to recognize their Messiah. Many of the priests, elders, and scribes were corrupt leaders who were guilty of despotic and hypocritical leadership. They were also guilty of becoming rich at the expense of the people.

3. The consequences of the condemned (v. 6)

"I will no more pity the inhabitants of the land, saith the Lord, but, lo, I will deliver the men, every one, into his neighbor's hand, and into the hand of his king; and they shall smite the land, and out of their hand I will not deliver them."

a) An absence of pity

It's sad that foreigners made merchandise out of Israel. It's even sadder that their own leaders didn't care enough to teach them the truths of God. But the saddest thing of all is that God Himself said He didn't pity them anymore. *Ichabod* was written over the nation because God departed from it (cf. 1 Sam. 4:21). Because His people would reject the Messiah, God would not pity them. Rather, He would deliver His people "into [their] neighbors' hand," indicative of the civil strife that occurred within the besieged city.

b) An absence of protection

The Lord also said He would deliver His people "into the hand of [their] king." Who was Israel's king in A.D. 70? Technically speaking, Israel had no king then, which might cause you to wonder how this prophecy could have been fulfilled in A.D. 70. They could have had a king when Jesus came, since as their Messiah He was and is the King of kings. But the people mocked Him. Pontius Pilate brought Jesus out before the people and mockingly said, "Behold, your King! But they cried out, Away with him, away with him, crucify him! Pilate saith unto them, Shall I crucify your King? The chief priests answered, We have no king but Caesar" (John 19:14-15). They made their awful choice and put themselves in the hand of Caesar, whose legions devoured them only a few decades later as a fulfillment of Zechariah's prophecy.

The Jewish leaders had concluded that if they didn't get rid of Jesus and the controversy surrounding Him, the Romans would intervene and take over completely (John 11:47-50). It is ironic that to avoid a

Roman takeover, they killed the real King—the very thing that ultimately brought about their destruction by the Roman army.

B. The Parable Enacted (vv. 7-14)

1. The role of the shepherd (v. 7)

a) His teaching (v. 7a)

"I will feed the flock of slaughter, even you, O poor of the flock."

Verse 7 resumes the thought of verse 4. Zechariah apparently carried out his role as a shepherd and started to teach the flock of Israel, but only the poor listened. That is a prophetic parable of what happened when Jesus came to feed the flock. He recognized that fact when He said, "Blessed are the poor in spirit" (Matt. 5:3). In 1 Corinthians 1:26 Paul says that among those who are saved, there are "not many mighty, not many noble."

The Hebrew word translated "poor" is used in an economic sense to refer to someone without any financial means. It is also used of someone who is physically afflicted with disease or socially afflicted with persecution because of his identification with God's people. It can refer to those who recognize their spiritual weakness. The poor in spirit—those who recognized their need of a Savior—accepted His teaching. The religious leaders didn't. Mark 12:37 tells us that when Jesus taught, "the common people heard him gladly." John 1:11-12 says, "He came unto his own, and his own received him not. But as many as received him, to them gave he power to become the children of God." It was the elect remnant of true believers who came to be fed by the Messiah and chose to follow Him. Commentator David Baron said, "He fed all; but the poor of the flock alone, those who were despised of men because they would not follow the pride of the high priests and scribes and Pharisees, believed on Him" (*The Visions & Prophecies of Zechariah* [Grand Rapids: Kregel, 1972], p. 392).

61

b) His tools (v. 7*b*)

> "I took unto me two staves; the one I called Beauty, and the other I called Bands; and I fed the flock."

Zechariah continues acting out the parable by taking two sticks. Shepherds often carried two sticks, which are identified in Psalm 23:4 as a rod and a staff. The rod was thicker than the staff. It was used for beating off wild beasts. The staff was for gently retrieving the sheep that got caught in difficult places.

The stick called "Beauty" means "graciousness," and the one called "Bands" means "unity," denoting a binding together of something. Christ the Good Shepherd expressed the love and grace of God by tenderly caring for His people, who were like sheep without a shepherd (Mark 6:34). Throughout His ministry our Lord demonstrated mercy and forgiveness.

The stick called "Bands" or "Unity" speaks of Jesus' unifying ministry. As the Messiah, He came to gather the lost sheep of the house of Israel into one fold (Matt. 15:24). It was in that spirit that He fed the flock of slaughter.

2. The rejection of the Shepherd (v. 8)

> "Three shepherds also I cut off in one month; and my soul loathed them, and their soul also abhorred me."

Verse 8 is difficult to interpret. I agree with those who say the three shepherds refer to the priests, elders, and scribes of Israel. I believe the Lord fulfilled the symbolism of bestowing grace and unity upon the populace, but when it came to the religious leaders He confronted their hypocrisy (Matt. 23). He "cut off" or disowned them with scathing denunciations. The time period of "one month" is best understood as referring to a short period of time.

"My soul loathed them" literally means "My soul was short with them," referring to the limits of God's patience toward the unrepentant. Therefore the phrase shouldn't be interpreted as referring to hatred. When Jesus came, He tried to gather His people into one fold, but the religious leaders repeatedly rejected Him and finally succeeded in crucifying Him.

3. The response of the Shepherd (vv. 9-14)

   a) Abandoning the unbelievers (v. 9)

   "Then said I, I will not feed you; that which dieth, let it die; and that which is to be cut off, let it be cut off; and let the rest eat, every one, the flesh of another."

   The Lord is telling those who refuse to believe that He will set them aside. The verse is reminiscent of Romans 1, which says that God gave them up to pursue their own sinful self-destruction. So the good Shepherd would gather in the poor (v. 7) but abandon the false religious leaders and all others who would not hear to their merciless enemies! That speaks of God's turning Israel over to the terrible judgment of A.D. 70. Josephus reported that during the siege, some of the starving inhabitants resorted to acts of cannibalism (*Wars* 6.3.4).

   b) Breaking the covenant (v. 10)

   "I took my staff, even Beauty, and cut it asunder, that I might break my covenant which I had made with all the peoples."

   God was saying that He would set aside His graciousness and cease His providential care for His people. Thus God allowed Rome to invade Israel.

   c) Confirming the word (v. 11)

   "It was broken in that day; and so the poor of the flock that waited upon me knew that it was the word of the Lord."

   In A.D. 70 the staff of Graciousness was shattered, and judgment came. "The poor of the flock" refers to the church, the believing community. Jesus warned them that God would judge the apostate Jewish nation (Luke 21:20-24). They were the ones who waited on the Lord, being submissive to His will. They knew judgment taking place was ordained by God.

d) Being betrayed by the people (vv. 12-13)

(1) The determination of the price (v. 12)

"I said unto them, If ye think good, give me my price; and if not, forbear. So they weighed for my price thirty pieces of silver."

So no one would think that God was too severe in His judgment of Israel, Zechariah prophetically enacted how His Shepherd would be treated. Jesus is pictured as asking those He came to shepherd what they felt He was worth to them. Although He came and healed the sick, raised the dead, taught the truth, and offered eternal life, the religious leaders valued Him at a mere thirty pieces of silver. Rather than ignore Him and give Him no price, the leaders mocked Him by offering the compensation paid for a slave that had been gored by an ox (Ex. 21:32). Their thinking that Jesus' ministry was worth a slave's price heightens the severity of their rejection. Their contemptible evaluation was worthy of severe judgment, because He was their King—the God of Israel in human flesh.

(2) The distribution to the potter (v. 13)

"The Lord said unto me, Cast it unto the potter—a lordly price that I was prized at of them. And I took the thirty pieces of silver, and cast them to the potter in the house of the Lord."

That's exactly what happened to the thirty pieces of silver that the chief priest paid Judas for betraying Jesus. Guilt-ridden Judas went back to the Temple and threw the blood money on the ground. The priests gathered the money and

used it to buy a field from a potter. That is recorded for us in Matthew 27:3-10. Only God could
predict such events.

e) Forsaking the nation (v. 14)

"Then I cut asunder mine other staff, even Bands,
that I might break the brotherhood between Judah
and Israel."

By symbolically breaking his staff of unity, Zechariah
was prophesying that God would destroy the nation.
When the Romans came in A.D. 70 many Jews were
killed. Many of those who didn't die directly at the
hands of the Romans died from starvation or at the
hands of their own despairing countrymen. Following the fall of Jerusalem, the children of Israel were
dissolved as a national entity and were dispersed.

The message of Zechariah is clear. Before the destruction of Jerusalem, God Himself would appear in the person of Jesus
Christ, the True Shepherd, and attempt to feed His flock of
slaughter. Only the poor of the flock would follow His Word,
and the rest, especially the leaders, would reject it. The good
Shepherd would have no more value to them than a common
slave. As a consequence the people were given over to severe
judgment, which included death, famine, war, civil strife, and
the destruction of the nation. The nation went out of existence,
and the Jewish people were scattered over the world because
they rejected the true Shepherd.

Focusing on the Facts

1. In what role does Zechariah picture the Messiah in chapter 11
   (see p. 54)?
2. Describe how the tone of chapter 11 differs from that of the
   previous chapters (see p. 54).
3. Why are the trees and shepherds in Israel pictured as wailing
   (vv. 1-3; see p. 55)?
4. To what historical incident does the devastation of verses 1-3
   refer (see p. 56)?

5. Although the Jews were scattered over the known world, how has God's sovereignty worked to their benefit (see pp. 56-57)?
6. Is verbalizing God's revelation the only means of prophesying? Explain (see p. 57).
7. What did God command Zechariah to do in verse 4 (see p. 57)?
8. Identify the "flock of slaughter." Why did God want to feed the flock destined for slaughter (see p. 58)?
9. Although God used other nations to judge Israel, does that mean they are not guilty? Explain (see p. 58).
10. What reaction did Israel's own leaders have toward the nation's impending judgment (v. 5; see p. 59)?
11. What did God say would be the consequences of Israel's rejection of their Messiah (v. 6; see p. 60)?
12. What king did the people of Israel automatically select when they rejected Jesus (John 19:14-15; see p. 60)?
13. What did the Jewish leaders do to avoid Roman intervention over the controversy surrounding Jesus? How did that backfire on them (see pp. 60-61)?
14. Identify the class of people who primarily responded to Jesus' teaching. Support your answer with Scripture (see p. 61).
15. Explain the significance of the two shepherds' staves of Zechariah (v. 7; see p. 62).
16. How did Jesus "cut off" the religious leaders who "abhorred" Him (v. 8; see p. 62)?
17. When the nation of Israel rejected their Messiah, how was God's graciousness set aside (v. 10; see p. 63)?
18. Who were "the poor of the flock" who recognized the fulfillment of prophecy in the fall of Jerusalem (v. 11; see pp. 63-64)?
19. Explain the significance of God's Shepherd being valued at thirty pieces of silver (v. 12; see p. 64).
20. Explain the symbolism of the staff of unity being broken (v. 14; see p. 65).

Pondering the Principles

1. Zechariah 11 paints a tragic scene of punishment. Those who witness and experience it wail as they see it approaching. As a just Judge, God rewards man "according to his deeds: to them who by patient continuance in well-doing seek for glory and honor and immortality, eternal life; but unto them that are contentious, and do not obey the truth, but obey unrighteousness, indignation and wrath" (Rom. 2:6-8). When you communicate

66

the gospel to others, do you warn them about God's judgment of sin and the consequences of rejecting the Good Shepherd? Consider using a passage such as 2 Thessalonians 1:7-10. Seek to have the mind-set of the apostle Paul, who, knowing the terror of the Lord, besought people to be reconciled to God (2 Cor. 5:11, 20).

2. Meditate on Isaiah 55. Identify the elements of God's nature expressed in that passage. Verse 6 urges the reader to seek the Lord "while he may be found [and] while he is near." Pray you might gain that sense of urgency in leading others to our merciful God.

5
The False Shepherd

Outline

Introduction
A. His Coming
  1. Spoken of by the apostles
  2. Alluded to by the Lord
  3. Foretold by the prophets
B. His Conspiracy
  1. Evidence of satanic conflict
  2. Expectations of satanic conflict
C. His Character
  1. An intellectual genius
  2. An outstanding orator
  3. A master politician
  4. A commercial wizard
  5. A military genius
  6. A religious leader

Review
  I. The Ravage of the Wailing Shepherds (vv. 1-3)
 II. The Rejection of the True Shepherd (vv. 4-14)

Lesson
III. The Reception of the False Shepherd (vv. 15-17)
  A. His Nature (v. 15)
  B. His Work (v. 16)
    1. Allowed by God (v. 16*a*)
    2. Avoided by neglect (v. 16*b*)
      a) "[He] shall not visit those that are cut off."
      b) "Neither shall seek the young one."
      c) "Nor heal that which is broken."
      d) "Nor feed that which standeth still."

3. Accomplished for personal gain (v. 16c)
      a) "He shall eat the flesh of the fat."
      b) "[He shall] tear their claws [hooves] in pieces."
C. His Punishment (v. 17)
   1. Symbolized
   2. Stated
      a) The court of condemnation
      b) The termination of tyranny
   3. Supported
      a) His power deployed
      b) His punishment delineated

Introduction

The book of Zechariah is of tremendous prophetic importance in viewing history from the time of Zechariah to the return of the Lord Jesus Christ. One of the most significant prophetic events is the rise of an individual commonly known as the Antichrist. Although that is not specifically his title in the Old Testament, it certainly fits him well. The apostle John said there were many antichrists present in his day (1 John 2:18), but he spoke of one who would be the most vehement adversary of God to ever live, apart from Satan himself (1 John 4:3).

As we come to Zechariah 11:15-17, we come face to face with this being. He's not a demon or a fallen angel but an evil person whom the prophet identifies as a foolish shepherd (v. 15). In verse 17 he is called an impostor (KJV, "idol," archaic for "pretender"). He is a false shepherd, a contrast to the true Shepherd, the Lord Jesus Christ.

The apostle John, writing in the first century to a wide circle of believers, said, "Little children . . . ye have heard that antichrist shall come" (1 John 2:18). The coming of the Antichrist was common knowledge.

A. His Coming

1. Spoken of by the apostles

The apostle Paul wrote specifically about the coming of this individual: "That man of sin [will] be revealed, the son of perdition" (2 Thess. 2:3).

2. Alluded to by the Lord

In John 5:43 Jesus says, "I am come in my Father's name, and ye receive me not; if another shall come in his own name, him ye will receive." Jesus was echoing the theme of Zechariah 11: that Israel would reject the true Shepherd and accept a false one. In Matthew 24 Jesus associated the coming of false prophets (the Antichrist will be the greatest false prophet) with the abomination of desolation, which will occur in the middle of the seven-year covenant he will establish with Israel (vv. 11-15; cf. Dan. 9:27).

3. Foretold by the prophets

One such prophecy is the text we're studying in this chapter, Zechariah 11:15-17. It reads, "The Lord said unto me, Take unto thee yet the instruments of a foolish shepherd; for, lo, I will raise up a shepherd in the land, who shall not visit those that are cut off, neither shall seek the young one, nor heal that which is broken, nor feed that which standeth still, but he shall eat the flesh of the fat, and tear their claws [hoofs] in pieces. Woe to the idol [false] shepherd that leaveth the flock! The sword shall be upon his arm, and upon his right eye; his arm shall be completely dried up, and his right eye shall be utterly darkened." That is one of several Old Testament passages referring to the Antichrist.

B. His Conspiracy

1. Evidence of satanic conflict

God and Satan have been at war ever since Satan fell. Before the world began, Satan sought to be God's equal, saying, "I will ascend into heaven . . . I will be like the Most High" (Isa. 14:13-14). God threw Satan out of heaven, and a host of the angels followed him. Since that time Satan and the other fallen angels have continued in their rebellion against God. The particular attack Satan has been concentrating on most since the Fall of man has been directed toward the seed promised in Genesis 3:15. That verse promises that a redeemer would fatally wound Satan, symbolized by the serpent. Therefore Satan did everything he could throughout history to stop that seed, who is the Messiah, from arriving. Because God chose Israel as the nation through which the Messiah would come, Satan has always tried to destroy Israel to prevent His establishing the kingdom. As the Messiah who has promised to return, Jesus Christ is still the object of Satan's attacks; and Israel, as the future recipient of many of God's promises, is still persecuted in our day.

a) The "sons of God"

Satan's first attempt to stop the messianic seed from coming was to try to corrupt the human race so that a sinless Messiah, needed to redeem a sinful human race, could never be born. Genesis 6:2 says that "the sons of God" (demons) cohabitated with "the daughters of men" (human women). Satan tried to produce a half-breed race of demonic humans. But Satan's attempt failed when God drowned that entire race in the flood, saving only Noah and his family.

b) Pharaoh

Satan again tried to destroy Israel through the pharaoh of Egypt, who commanded that all male babies born to Israelites be killed. But again God preserved the people of Israel and delivered them out of Egypt by the hand of one man who wasn't slaughtered as a baby: Moses. Satan's efforts were thwarted again.

c) Mordecai

The book of Esther records that Satan ultimately tried to wipe out the entire nation of Israel while they were captives in Persia. Through the wisdom and bravery of Mordecai and Esther, the Jewish people were saved from wholesale slaughter.

d) Herod

In the New Testament we read that Herod the Great tried to slaughter every male child under two in the region of Bethlehem to eliminate the prophesied King of the Jews, whom he feared would usurp his throne. But God enabled Jesus the Messiah to escape.

e) Satan

When Jesus began His ministry, Satan tried to thwart Him with temptation. But he failed again.

f) The Nazarenes

The people of Nazareth wanted to push Jesus off a cliff for claiming to be the Messiah, but He passed through the midst of them and escaped unharmed (Luke 4:16-30).

g) The religious leaders

Finally Satan succeeded in having Christ nailed to a cross and sealed in a tomb. But that failed, because Christ rose from the grave.

2. Expectations of satanic conflict

Satan is a loser. He's failed every attempt he's made to destroy God's people and their Messiah. But he stubbornly continues to oppose God in this present age. Ephesians 6:12 says, "We wrestle not against flesh and blood, but against principalities, against powers, against the rulers of the darkness of this world, against spiritual wickedness in high places." We're in a battle against demonic forces and Satan himself. And the war rages on. But Christ assures us in Matthew 16:18, saying, "I will build my church, and the gates of hades shall not prevail against it." The assumption is that the gates of hell are trying to overcome God's kingdom.

There's coming a time when Satan will pull off another attack. Revelation 12 prophesies about the war Satan and his demons will wage against Michael the archangel and the holy angels. It will be a war beyond anything we could ever imagine. When Michael and the angels win, God will cast Satan and his host to earth. There they will spawn their evil in an unprecedented manner during what is known as the Tribulation, again trying to destroy Israel and prevent her Messiah from returning. His chief agent will be the Antichrist. This man's task will be to set up a world government of evil and eliminate God's people and their returning Messiah.

C. His Character

1. An intellectual genius

Daniel 7:8 describes him as having "eyes like the eyes of a man" (cf. v. 20). The eye is often a symbol of intelligence.

2. An outstanding orator

Daniel 7:8 says the Antichrist will have "a mouth speaking great things" (cf. v. 20). Effective leadership is predicated on the ability to communicate.

3. A master politician

Revelation 6:2 says he will conquer the world having a bow without any arrows. That means he'll conquer peacefully through politics. The world will be looking for someone to bring peace and economic stability. Daniel 11:21 says, "In his estate shall stand up a vile person [the Antichrist], to whom they shall not give the honor of the kingdom; but he shall come in peaceably, and obtain the kingdom by flatteries."

4. A commercial wizard

Daniel 8:25 says, "Through his policy . . . he shall cause deceit to prosper in his hand; and he shall magnify himself in his heart, and by peace shall destroy many; he shall stand up against the Prince of princes, but he shall be broken without hand." He will be a wizard at building a world system of economics that feeds his own pocket (cf. Rev. 18).

5. A military genius

According to Daniel 7:23 he "shall devour the whole earth, and shall tread it down, and break it in pieces." He will be a military leader without equal. He's going to be everything that Nebuchadnezzar, Alexander the Great, the Caesars, and Napoleon Bonaparte were in terms of military ability combined in one individual. Revelation 13:4, 7 says, "They worshiped the beast [the Antichrist], saying, Who is like the beast? Who is able to make war with him? . . . It was given unto him to make war with the saints, and to overcome them; and power was given him over all kindreds, and tongues, and nations." The Antichrist will conquer the world.

6. A religious leader

Second Thessalonians 2:3-4 identifies him as the "man of sin . . . the son of perdition, who opposeth and exalteth himself above all that is called God, or that is worshiped, so that he, as God, sitteth in the temple of God, showing himself that he is God." He will command the whole world to worship him.

The Antichrist will be Satan's final effort to thwart Christ from returning and establishing His kingdom. We don't know who he is, but we do know what the Bible says about him. It's amazing to think that our sophisticated world, with its religious, social, political, and economic diversity, could agree on one leader. But somehow the world will be so ready for him it will fall at his feet. He will even be able to deceive the nation of Israel—as independent as it now is of other nations—and bring it under his power with the rest of the world.

I believe the Antichrist will come out of a revived Roman Empire because Daniel 9:26 says, "The people of the prince that shall come shall destroy the city and the sanctuary." The people who destroyed Jerusalem were the Romans in A.D. 70. That implies the Antichrist will be a Gentile from Europe. Daniel 9:27 implies he will make a covenant with Israel for the seven-year period known as the Tribulation. In the midst of it he will violate that covenant and desecrate the Temple, demanding that everyone worship him. That is what Jesus refers to in Matthew 24:15 as "the abomination of desolation, spoken of by Daniel the prophet."

The Antichrist will begin slaughtering believers during the last half of the Tribulation. Jesus warned that those who witness it should immediately "flee into the mountains" (v. 16). So many people will be killed that if God had not set a limit to the reign of the Antichrist, everyone would die (v. 22). The Antichrist will have total control over the world. Through him Satan will amass the world's strength against Christ when He returns to establish His kingdom at the end of the Tribulation.

Review

I. THE RAVAGE OF THE WAILING SHEPHERDS (vv. 1-3; see pp. 54-57)

II. THE REJECTION OF THE TRUE SHEPHERD (vv. 4-14; see pp. 57-65)

Lesson

III. THE RECEPTION OF THE FALSE SHEPHERD (vv. 15-17)

The irony of Israel's rejecting the true Shepherd is that they end up receiving a false one. But he wouldn't appear until centuries later after Zechariah was written. Zechariah 11 jumps from A.D. 70 (v. 14) to the Great Tribulation in the end times (v. 15).

A. His Nature (v. 15)

"The Lord said unto me, Take unto thee yet the instruments of a foolish shepherd."

Having just played the part of Christ, Zechariah now plays the part of the Antichrist. "The instruments of a foolish shepherd" might have been a broken staff or a club with metal on it used to beat stubborn sheep into submission. Whatever the instruments were, they would clearly be inappropriate for a shepherd who wanted to tenderly care for his sheep.

The Hebrew word translated "foolish" in the Old Testament is a synonym for "wicked." The book of Proverbs in many places equates the wicked person with the fool. Proverbs 5:22-23 says, "His own iniquities shall take the wicked himself, and he shall be held with the cords of his sins. He shall die without instruction, and in the greatness of his folly he shall go astray." Psalm 14:1 says, "The fool hath said in his heart, There is no God." The fool lives in rebellion against God. Foolishness doesn't mean that he's mentally incompetent but that he is wicked.

The world will willingly accept the Antichrist as its shepherd but will recognize too late that he doesn't carry a staff in his hand but a club. He will allow the false church to exist (Rev. 17:1-6) once the true church has been raptured and taken to heaven. He will slaughter not only the false church after a period of toleration (Rev. 17:7-18) but also two-thirds of the Jewish people (Zech. 13:8).

B. His Work (v. 16)

1. Allowed by God (v. 16*a*)

"For, lo, I will raise up a shepherd in the land."

Notice it is God who permits the wicked shepherd to arise. Nothing ever happens outside His sovereign plan. God is no victim. He is not biting His nails, hoping everything goes all well, or second-guessing Satan. He will allow the Antichrist to do what he will do just as He allowed Satan to afflict Job within the boundaries He had set.

2. Avoided by neglect (v. 16*b*)

a) "[He] shall not visit those that are cut off."

The Antichrist will not seek out sheep who have been separated from the flock and are therefore vulnerable to the elements and wild beasts. The true shepherd goes out and finds the sheep that have been isolated or wounded, but this one doesn't even bother to look for them, because the flock's welfare is not his concern.

b) "Neither shall seek the young one."

The foolish shepherd has no concern for the little lambs who get lost and cannot keep up with the flock. The true shepherd, however, leaves the ninety-nine to find the one that's lost (Luke 15:4).

c) "Nor heal that which is broken."

Frequently a sheep would break a leg, so the good shepherd would make a splint to allow the leg to heal. The foolish shepherd will not be interested in salving the wounds of his sheep.

d) "Nor feed that which standeth still."

This refers to the strong sheep who require a minimum amount of help. They don't have to be chased, found, or mended. Nothing needs to be done except feed them, but the foolish shepherd doesn't even do that. To the strong who need the least help, he is no help at all. To the weak, wounded, lost, and dying, he is absolutely indifferent.

If you were watching Zechariah perform this parable you'd say, "This is a terrible shepherd!" He is the opposite of everything he should be. But the prophet isn't through yet. Although the foolish shepherd fails to do what he should do, he also does some things that he shouldn't do.

3. *Accomplished for personal gain (v. 16c)*

a) "He shall eat the flesh of the fat."

The foolish shepherd will eat the fat sheep from his
own flock. He is greedy and selfish, devouring his
sheep rather than feeding them. When the Antichrist
comes, it will be all hearts and flowers for three-and-
a-half years until the abomination of desolation takes
place. Then he will devour Israel in an unprecedented slaughter. Zechariah 13:8-9 says, "It shall come to
pass that in all the land, saith the Lord, two parts in it
shall be cut off and die; but the third shall be left in it.
And I will bring the third part through the fire, and
will refine them as silver is refined, and will test them
as gold is tested." The Antichrist will kill two-thirds
of the people in Israel (Zech. 13:8). Only God in His
mercy spares one-third of Israel, hiding them away in
Edom (Rev. 12:6). He will also kill those Gentiles who
become believers during the Tribulation and refuse to
take his mark (Rev. 7:9-14; 20:4).

b) "[He shall] tear their claws [hooves] in pieces."

If you ever ate spare ribs or a T-bone steak when you
were really hungry, you probably cleaned off the
bone to get at every last morsel. That is the picture in
this verse. The Antichrist will not only eat the flesh of
the fat sheep, but he will tear their hooves to pieces
to consume every last bit.

No doubt the people in Zechariah's day were shocked
by this characterization of a shepherd who would do absolutely the opposite of what they expected. But ironically that is the shepherd they will choose during the
Tribulation. They turned their back on the real One and
will receive a foolish one.

I have a great love for Israel. When I meet Jewish peo-
ple, I often tell them that my best friends are Jewish—
Abraham, Moses, David, Jesus, Paul, Peter, James, and
John! I almost wish I were Jewish and could become a

believer during the Tribulation so that I could have the thrill of recognizing my Messiah and entering the earthly kingdom in my physical body. (But being raptured with the church and returning with Christ in a glorified body is just as exciting to look forward to!)

Sadly, before the day of Israel's salvation there's going to come a terrible period when they line up with the wrong ruler. In spite of their great hope and confidence in him, he will devour them down to the hoof.

C. His Punishment (v. 17)

"Woe to the idol [worthless] shepherd that leaveth the flock! The sword shall be upon his arm, and upon his right eye; his arm shall be completely dried up, and his right eye shall be utterly darkened."

1. Symbolized

"Woe" signifies a curse. Zechariah condemns the worthless shepherd who will forsake the flock. God will come with a sword of judgment and cut off his right arm, a symbol of strength. The Antichrist's power will be torn away from him. His right eye, probably a reference to intelligence, will be darkened to the point of mental incompetency, and he will shrivel under the judgment of God.

2. Stated

a) The court of condemnation

This judgment upon the Antichrist is also prophesied in Daniel 7. After abusing his power and persecuting the people of God, the Antichrist will have to answer to God. Verses 9-10 say, "I beheld till the thrones were placed, and the Ancient of days did sit, whose garment was white as snow, and the hair of his head like pure wool; his throne was like the fiery flame, and his wheels as burning fire. A fiery stream issued and came forth from before him; a thousand thousands ministered unto him, and ten thousand times ten thousand stood before him; the judgment was set, and the books were opened." Daniel envisioned God in all of His majestic glory, surrounded by the angelic host.

b) The termination of tyranny

Daniel 7:11-12 says, "I beheld then because of the voice of the great words which the horn [Antichrist] spoke; I beheld even till the beast was slain, and its body destroyed, and given to the burning flame. As for the rest of the beasts, they had their dominion taken away, yet their lives were prolonged for a season and time." Daniel's vision of four beasts (vv. 1-8) represented the Babylonian, Medo-Persian, Greek, and Roman empires. They were all eventually conquered, but they still retained a measure of their influence. However, in the case of the revived Roman Empire, the Antichrist will be destroyed with no dominion remaining. He will lose his power and his life at the same time.

Daniel 7:24-27 gives an angelic interpretation of Daniel's vision earlier in the chapter. "The ten horns out of this kingdom [the revived Roman Empire] are ten kings that shall arise; and another shall rise after them" (v. 24). Ten rulers will head a ten-nation confederacy of the revived Roman Empire, which significantly parallels the European Common Market of today. From among them the Antichrist will arise and "he shall speak great words against the Most High, and shall wear out the saints . . . and they shall be given into his hand until a time and times and the dividing of time" (v. 25). In other words, the Antichrist will blaspheme God and slaughter His people for three-and-a-half years. But then his reign will end: "The judgment shall sit; and they shall take away his dominion, to consume and destroy it unto the end" (v. 26). Christ will come in judgment upon the Antichrist and his government and will establish God's earthly kingdom.

3. Supported

a) His power deployed

Daniel 8:23-24 says, "In the latter time of their kingdom, when the transgressors are come to the full, a king of fierce countenance, and understanding dark sentences, shall stand up. And his power shall be mighty, but not by his own power; and he shall destroy wonderfully, and shall prosper, and continue, and shall destroy the mighty and the holy people." The Antichrist, also designated in Daniel as "the little horn" (7:8) and "the prince that shall come" (9:26), will have incredible power because behind him is Satan. His destruction will be so intense that people will be in awe of it.

b) His punishment delineated

Daniel 8:25 says, "He shall also stand up against the Prince of princes, but he shall be broken without hand." When the Antichrist opposes Christ Himself, who returns as the Prince of princes, the King of kings and Lord of lords (Rev. 19:16), there won't even be a struggle—he'll be shattered. Revelation 19:20 reiterates the judgment upon the Antichrist and his cohort: "The beast was taken, and with him the false prophet. . . . These both were cast alive into a lake of fire burning with brimstone." Revelation 20:10 says, "The devil that deceived them was cast into the lake of fire and brimstone, where the beast and the false prophet are, and shall be tormented day and night forever and ever." The Antichrist's dominion will be destroyed. He will be tormented in hell throughout eternity with Satan and all those who occupy Satan's kingdom. God will severely judge the false shepherd of Zechariah 11.

Focusing on the Facts

1. Apart from Satan himself, who is the most vehement adversary of God that will ever live (see p. 70)?

2. Why was the coming of the Antichrist common knowledge among the early Christians (see pp. 70-71)?
3. Explain the promise of Genesis 3:15 and why it has caused Satan to focus his attack on Israel (see p. 72).
4. What was Satan's first attempt in preventing the Messiah from coming (Gen. 6:2; see p. 72)?
5. Give a biblical example of how Satan tried to destroy Israel. Also, give an example of how he tried to prevent Christ from fulfilling His work of redemption (see pp. 72-73).
6. In spite of Satan's continued attempts to oppose God and His people, how do we know that he will never ultimately succeed (Matt. 16:18; see p. 73)?
7. When will Satan begin to spawn his evil in an unprecedented manner (see p. 74)?
8. Although he will have tremendous military backing, how will the Antichrist apparently take over the world (Dan. 11:21; see p. 74)?
9. In what sense will the Antichrist be a religious leader (2 Thess. 2:3-4; see p. 75)?
10. What is amazing about our sophisticated society agreeing to follow the Antichrist (see p. 75)?
11. What indicates that the Antichrist will arise out of a revived Roman Empire (Dan. 9:26; see p. 75)?
12. How will the Antichrist violate his covenant with Israel (see pp. 75-76)?
13. What is the irony of Israel's rejection of the true Shepherd (see p. 76)?
14. How was Zechariah told to characterize the Antichrist (v. 15; see p. 77)?
15. According to verse 16, who allows the Antichrist to arise (see p. 77)?
16. What will the Antichrist neglect to do (v. 16b; see p. 78)?
17. Explain what the Antichrist will do for his personal gain (v. 16c; see p. 79).
18. How does verse 17 symbolize judgment upon the Antichrist (see p. 80)?
19. After the Antichrist is judged in the presence of the Ancient of days in Daniel 7, what fate does he encounter (Dan. 7:12; see pp. 80-81)?
20. What can be seen as a modern-day parallel of the ten kings who will precede the arrival of the Antichrist (see p. 81)?
21. According to Revelation 19:20 and 20:10, where does the Antichrist spend eternity (see p. 82)?

Pondering the Principles

1. It is easy to get caught up in the speculations that often surround end-time events and lose our focus on Christ. Some of the Thessalonians were "shaken in mind" and "troubled" because they believed they had missed the rapture (2 Thess. 2:2). Paul never had an attitude of being so heavenly minded that he was no earthly good. Rather, he could say at the end of his life, "I have fought a good fight, I have finished my course, I have kept the faith; henceforth there is laid up for me a crown of righteousness, which the Lord, the righteous judge, shall give me at that day; and not to me only, but unto all them also that love his appearing" (2 Tim. 4:7-8). Commit those verses to memory, and determine your focus.

2. It's easy to be emotionally overwhelmed when considering the intense evil of Satan and the Antichrist. But praise God that the devastation of the Tribulation will end when "the Sun of righteousness [rises] with healing in his wings" (Mal. 4:2). Let this stanza from "A Mighty Fortress Is Our God," by Martin Luther, encourage you:

> And though this world, with devils filled, should
> threaten to undo us,
> We will not fear, for God hath willed His truth to
> triumph through us.
> The Prince of Darkness grim, we tremble not for
> him;
> His rage we can endure, for lo, his doom is sure;
> One little word shall fell him.

Thank the Lord for enabling us to have victory in the spiritual battles we encounter daily.

3. Sadly, the dark cloud of judgment can never be removed from Jewish people who have died rejecting Christ. Ask the Lord to help you reach out to those who still have time to embrace their Messiah, telling them that their true Shepherd still loves them and wants them as His sheep. Praise God also for His mercy in one day regathering His people, even though they will align themselves with the false shepherd.

6
Israel's Final Deliverance

Outline

Introduction

Lesson
I. The Siege of Israel (vv. 1-3)
   A. The Burden for Israel (v. 1)
      1. Its object
      2. Its source
   B. The Battle in Israel (vv. 2-3)
      1. The symbolism explained
         a) Intoxication
         b) Injury
      2. The setting examined
         a) The attack described
         b) The armies identified
            (1) The army from the west
            (2) The army from the north
            (3) The army from the south
            (4) The army from the east
         c) The aftermath depicted
         d) The adversaries destroyed
II. The Shielding of Israel (vv. 4-9)
   A. The Panic of the Defiant (v. 4)
   B. The Preservation of the Defenseless (v. 5)
   C. The Paradox of the Defeated (v. 6)
   D. The Priority of Deliverance (v. 7)
   E. The Power of David (v. 8)
   F. The Promise of Destruction (v. 9)

Introduction

The twelfth chapter of Zechariah presents the familiar theme of Israel's final deliverance and salvation. Zechariah has been predicting it throughout and now gives a description of its coming to pass.

Today it is relatively easy to imagine Israel as the focal point of the world. I imagine if we had been living a hundred years ago that would seem somewhat obscure. But since its reappearance as a nation in 1948, the eyes of the world have focused on Israel. Seemingly indomitable, it exists as an island in a sea of nations endeavoring to drown it. God is not yet finished with Israel. The Bible teaches that there is coming a great day for the nation of Israel—a day of tremendous spiritual salvation and political victory. That has been prophesied repeatedly in the Old and New Testaments and is detailed for us in Zechariah 12. The tragic history of Israel will be reversed to culminate in a future of unprecedented joy. This chapter is full of truths that are exciting not only for anyone who is Jewish but also for anyone who knows that God is in control of history.

Lesson

I. THE SIEGE OF ISRAEL (vv. 1-3)

"The burden of the word of the Lord for Israel, saith the Lord, who stretcheth forth the heavens, and layeth the foundation of the earth, and formeth the spirit of man within him. Behold, I will make Jerusalem a cup of trembling unto all the peoples round about, when they shall be in the siege both against Judah and against Jerusalem. And in that day will I make Jerusa-

86

lem a burdensome stone for all peoples; all that burden themselves with it shall be cut in pieces, though all the nations of the earth be gathered together against it."

A. The Burden for Israel (v. 1)

1. Its object

This prophecy is directed toward Israel. It begins by describing a siege against the nation. A siege is a military attack by an army, usually in the form of a blockade, against a city. There will be a great attack by the Gentile nations against Israel in the future. It will be another world war—the battle of the centuries, the greatest war of history. It is commonly referred to as the Battle of Armageddon. All the nations of the world will converge on Israel in an effort to destroy it and prevent the Messiah's return to establish His kingdom.

Verse 1 says this is "the burden of the word of the Lord for Israel." More specifically, verse 2 says this is directed toward Judah and Jerusalem. That is supported through such phrases as "the governors of Judah" (vv. 5-6), "the inhabitants of Jerusalem" (vv. 5, 7-8, 10), "the tents of Judah" (v. 7), and "the house of David" (vv. 8, 10).

The Hebrew word translated "burden" comes from a term that is used frequently in prophetic literature. It's used in Zechariah 9:1 for a prophecy against the Gentiles. It signifies a prophecy of grief or anxiety that burdens the prophet who is obliged to proclaim it and the people who must receive it. There's going to be grief before there will be wholesale repentance and conversion in Israel.

2. Its source

Furthermore, the burden is from God Himself. He is proclaiming in the first person through Zechariah what He will do. He says, "Behold, I will make" (v. 2), "in that day will I make" (v. 3), "I will smite . . . and I will open mine eyes" (v. 4), and "in that day will I make" (v. 6). God sovereignly directs the course of events of history, whether through raising up a false shepherd or establishing His messianic kingdom.

God is making a promise that in spite of a siege set against Israel, He will bring about the deliverance and salvation of His people. His active role is emphasized so that those who hear this prophecy will have the confidence to believe it will come to pass. It doesn't depend on men but upon an unchanging God, who doesn't make plans and scuttle them and who isn't thwarted by some other power. When God plans to do something, it will be done. To confirm that ultimate power rests with God, verse 1 reminds us that He is the One "who stretcheth forth the heavens, and layeth the foundation of the earth, and formeth the spirit of man within him." The point is beautifully made that the God who made history will be the One to bring it to a close. That truth is a solid basis for confidence in the ultimate destiny of history.

The divine element is expressed in three ways in verse 1. First, "burden of the word of the Lord" indicates a divine message involving judgment. Second, "saith the Lord" specifically indicates that this is a message from God. Third, the description of God as the omnipotent Creator of the world emphasizes that He is in control of history.

B. The Battle in Israel (vv. 2-3)

1. The symbolism explained

Verses 2 and 3 are parallels. They begin with God's making Jerusalem "a cup of trembling" and "a burdensome stone," respectively, and state that the future siege of Jerusalem will make an impact on "all the peoples."

a) Intoxication

"Cup of trembling" refers to a large basin everyone can drink from (Heb., *saph*) rather than an individual cup (Heb., *kos*). This verse pictures the nations as a person who drinks too much wine and finds himself staggering. The trembling is not associated with nervousness but with intoxication.

When the nations converge on Israel and besiege Jerusalem, they will find themselves as ineffective as a drunkard trying to walk a straight line. By the time the nations make their way to Jerusalem, they will become figuratively drunk with their overinflated sense of power. Their overconfidence will so disorient them that they will be unable to claim their coveted prize, becoming easy prey for divine judgment. Revelation 17:6 is another example of a figurative use of drunkenness. It mentions that Satan's evil world system will become drunk "with the blood of the martyrs of Jesus."

b) Injury

Verse 3 presents a second metaphor: that of "a burdensome stone" (lit., "a stone of burden"). That refers to a heavy stone that was used in weightlifting contests. The analogy is simple. Like a heavy weight, Jerusalem will give a hernia to any nation that tries to gain victory over it. The phrase "shall be cut in pieces" is best understood in context to mean they shall grievously injure themselves. It refers to a rupture or other internal injuries sustained from lifting something too heavy. The proud Gentile nations won't be able to subdue Israel.

2. The setting examined

The phrase "in that day" refers to the time during the Tribulation when the nations gather together to besiege Jerusalem. It's an eschatological term that is also referred to as "the day of the Lord." The attacking nations will find themselves reeling around in a drunken stupor of confusion and irreparably injured because they try to do something that's impossible—destroy the people of God.

Zechariah's prophecy is not a fairy tale. A day is coming when the entire world will attack the nation of Israel and lose. Those are staggering odds, but having God on their side means that if the same people could bring down the walls of Jericho by blowing horns and marching around the city, then we cannot discount what will happen in the future.

a) The attack described

Other passages in the Bible also outline the battle of Armageddon for us. Joel 3:9-17 says, "Proclaim this among the nations, Prepare war, wake up the mighty men, let all the men of war draw near; let them come up; beat your plowshares into swords, and your pruning hooks into spears; let the weak say, I am strong. Assemble yourselves, and come, all ye nations, and gather yourselves together round about; there cause thy mighty ones to come down, O Lord. Let the nations be wakened, and come up to the Valley of Jehoshaphat; for there I will sit to judge all the nations round about. Put in the sickle; for the harvest is ripe; come, get down; for the press is full, the vats overflow; for their wickedness is great. Multitudes, multitudes in the valley of decision; for the day of the Lord is near in the valley of decision. The sun and the moon shall be darkened, and the stars shall withdraw their shining. The Lord also shall roar out of Zion, and utter his voice from Jerusalem, and the heavens and the earth shall shake; but the Lord will be the hope of his people, and the strength of the children of Israel. So shall ye know that I am the Lord, your God, dwelling in Zion, my holy mountain; then shall Jerusalem be holy."

But before Jerusalem becomes holy, the nations will come against Israel in a great war instigated by Satan, yet in direct accord with the plan of God. While their armies are surrounding Jerusalem, Jesus Christ will return and defeat them, judging them for their evil.

b) The armies identified

There are four armies represented at Armageddon.

(1) The army from the west (Dan. 7:7-8, 24; Rev. 17:12-14)

This army is known as the European Confederacy, the revived Roman Empire, which is made up of ten nations whose boundaries were once contained within the ancient Roman Empire. It will be led by the Antichrist, who will be the emperor of that particular dominion.

(2) The army from the north (Ezek. 38:1-6, 14-16)

This army is best identified as the Soviet Union (Magog) and her allies—Persia, Cush, Put, Gomer, and Togarmah, which are ancient names of modern Arab states.

(3) The army from the south (Dan. 11:40-44)

This army will be Egypt and her Arab allies.

(4) The army from the east (Rev. 9:13-16; 16:12-16)

This army of two hundred million soldiers will march toward Israel over the Euphrates River, which will be dried up at that time. Until this century, that was an inconceivable number. However, *Time* magazine in 1965 reported that Red China had a two-hundred-million-man militia (21 May 1965, p. 35).

c) The aftermath depicted

Revelation 14:20 says, "The winepress was trodden outside the city, and blood came out of the winepress, even unto the horse bridles, by the space of a thousand and six hundred furlongs." Apparently the four armies are nearly slaughtered outside the city of Jerusalem as they attempt to bring about a holocaust throughout the countryside. The unprecedented bloodshed will be so severe that it is symbolized as deep as a horse's bridle for two hundred miles. The whole land of Israel is going to be drowning in a blood bath as the battle rages.

d) The adversaries destroyed

The armies will become drunk with their assumed success but will be unable to claim their prize. Instead of victory, they will receive a political rupture in trying to lift a stone that's too heavy because God, so to speak, happens to be sitting on it. We see hope for the besieged city expressed in Psalm 118: "The Lord is on my side; I will not fear. What can man do unto me? The Lord taketh my part with those who help me; therefore shall I see my desire upon those who hate me. . . . All nations compassed me about, but in the name of the Lord will I destroy them. They compassed me about; yea, they compassed me about, but in the name of the Lord I will destroy them. They compassed me about like bees; they are quenched like the fire of thorns, for in the name of the Lord I will destroy them" (vv. 6-7, 10-12). That psalm attests to the victory that God will bring to Israel over the armies of Armageddon.

II. THE SHIELDING OF ISRAEL (vv. 4-9)

A. The Panic of the Defiant (v. 4)

"In that day, saith the Lord, I will smite every horse with terror, and his rider with madness; and I will open mine eyes upon the house of Judah, and will smite every horse of the peoples with blindness."

God is comforting His people, explaining that He will protect them in that day. Since horses were the symbol of strength in ancient times, verse 4 emphasizes God's superior power over Israel's enemies as He smites the horses with terror and confusion. Furthermore, He inflicts their riders with madness, putting them into a wild and helpless state of panic.

When the great armies of the world converge on Jerusalem, their weapons and soldiers will be rendered helpless. Although they will believe victory is at hand as they attack the seemingly vanquished Jews, they will find themselves rushing to their own destruction. The phrase "I will open mine eyes upon the house of Judah" assures Israel that He will be concerned and actively involved in what's happening to His people. God will open His eyes of love and forgiveness toward Israel as He brings about their deliverance.

B. The Preservation of the Defenseless (v. 5)

"The governors of Judah shall say in their heart, The inhabitants of Jerusalem shall be my strength in the Lord of hosts, their God."

The people in Israel who lived outside the city of Jerusalem were the most vulnerable in war in ancient times, being without the protection of fortified city walls. But knowing that God had chosen Jerusalem to be the city of His special affection will give confidence to future denizens of the surrounding countryside. They will recognize that they have been preserved because God has chosen Jerusalem. His promises to Jerusalem, which is the heart of the nation, will assure them of their divine invincibility. Perhaps they'll sing Psalm 46:5, which says of Jerusalem, "God is in the midst of her; she shall not be moved."

Zechariah 12:5 opens the door a crack to allow the light of saving faith to shine through. Many times in the nation's past, the people of Israel have assumed their strength was in themselves. But during the Tribulation they will come to recognize that their strength is not in their military prowess but in the Lord of hosts. They will turn from politics to God.

C. The Paradox of the Defeated (v. 6)

"In that day will I make the governors of Judah like an hearth of fir among the wood, and like a torch of fire in a sheaf; and they shall devour all the peoples round about, on the right hand and on the left; and Jerusalem shall be inhabited again in her own place, even in Jerusalem."

Living in a day of thermostats and forced-air heating, you may not know what a hearth or firepot is. It is a metal pot you put coals in to start a fire. If you put hot coals from a firepot on a pile of kindling, you would quickly start a fire. Similarly, a flame set to a dry sheaf of grain would ignite quickly. The prophecy compares the Gentile armies to kindling or sheaves and the governors of Judah as firepots or torches that devour wood. The relatively weak and outnumbered leaders of Israel are going to devour their enemies "round about on the right hand and on the left." That will allow Jerusalem to "be inhabited again in her own place." In the final battle nothing will be able to ultimately destroy the city of Jerusalem, which shall again be peacefully inhabited.

D. The Priority of Deliverance (v. 7)

"The Lord also shall save the tents of Judah first, that the glory of the house of David and the glory of the inhabitants of Jerusalem do not magnify themselves against Judah."

God will first deliver the defenseless country people. That will show those in the well-defended capital, which is delivered last, that the battle was not won by their military might or strategy.

E. The Power of David (v. 8)

"In that day shall the Lord defend the inhabitants of Jerusalem; and he that is feeble among them at that day shall be like David; and the house of David shall be like God, like the angel of the Lord before them."

The greatest soldier in the history of Israel was David. In fact, after he had killed Goliath and defeated the Philistines, the Israelites compared him to their first king, saying, "Saul hath slain his thousands; David his ten thousands" (1 Sam. 18:7). So if the weak will be like David, you can imagine what an incredible army Israel will have. The strong—represented by the house of David—will be like God. More specifically they'll be like the angel of the Lord, who is Christ. They will be infused with the energy of the Messiah Himself, implying that He will be there leading His people to victory. The angel of the Lord identifies Him as God Himself, namely the second Person of the Trinity.

This will be an exciting time that raptured believers will likely be able to witness. Believers will come out of heaven with Christ on white horses and have a perfect view (Rev. 19:14). At the climax of the Battle of Armageddon, Jesus Christ and this heavenly army will strengthen the people of Israel to conquer their enemies.

F. The Promise of Destruction (v. 9)

"It shall come to pass, in that day, that I will seek to destroy all the nations that come against Jerusalem."

God is going to wipe out those who seek to attack His people. The Hebrew term translated "will seek" speaks of the concentration of the marksman, who focuses on his target without being distracted. Revelation 16 and 19 chronicle the wrath of God and the judgment of Christ as He comes out of heaven in glory and power to conquer His foes.

Zechariah 12:1-9 prophetically describes Israel's great deliverance and the destruction of the armies of the world gathered against her. That's a political victory that will cause Israel and her enemies to recognize God at work. Verse 10 now makes a transition into the spiritual transformation of Israel.

III. THE SORROW OF ISRAEL (vv. 10b-14)

"They [Israel] shall look upon me whom they have pierced, and they shall mourn for him, as one mourneth for his only son, and shall be in bitterness for him, as one that is in bitterness for his firstborn. In that day shall there be a great mourning in Jerusalem, as the mourning of Hadadrimmon, in the Valley of Megiddon. And the land shall mourn, every family apart; the family of the house of David apart, and their wives apart; the family of the house of Nathan apart, and their wives apart; the family of the house of Levi apart, and their wives apart; the family of Shimei apart, and their wives apart; all the families that remain, every family apart, and their wives apart."

A. Its Cause

While Israel's spiritual eyes are focused on God and His deliverance, they will see God incarnate, their Lord and

Savior Jesus Christ coming as their victor—the very One they once rejected. That realization will cause national mourning among every family and individual. The Hebrew word translated "mourn" means "to strike the breast in deep grief." That men will mourn apart from their wives indicates individual acts of repentance that permeate the entire nation. How ironic that after winning their greatest victory they will mourn. But that's the anguish of true repentance.

The One Sin a Person Must Repent Of

Jesus said, "When [the Holy Spirit] is come, he will reprove the world of sin . . . because they believe not on me" (John 16:8-9). Unbelief is the one sin the Spirit of God must convict a person of to bring him to salvation. That's the sin the people of Israel will feel convicted of when they look on Christ, whom they once crucified. That's where salvation begins—in turning from rejecting Jesus Christ to believing in Him.

B. Its Comparison

The mourning and bitterness Israel will experience at that time is similar to that which took place when the righteous king Josiah was mortally wounded at Hadadrimmon in the valley of Megiddo. (Although not mentioned in 2 Chronicles 35:20-24, the scriptural account of Josiah's defeat, the name *Hadadrimmon* was apparently preserved by tradition and later recorded by Zechariah.) Pharaoh Neco of Egypt killed Josiah in battle, and the nation of Judah mourned its great loss. Zechariah prophesied that the mourning of Jerusalem and Israel in the day that Christ returns will be reminiscent of the mourning over the death of King Josiah.

C. Its Contrast

Commentator David Baron explains the singling out of the families of David, Nathan, Levi, and Shimei: "Through these . . . aristocratic and privileged lines, the rulers and the priests, who, alas! in times past often set an evil example to the whole nation, will now be foremost in their self-contrition and mourning over the great national sin, their

96

example for good will now also be followed by all the rest of the people" (*The Vision & Prophecies of Zechariah* [Grand Rapids: Kregel, 1972], p. 453).

Israel's deep mourning reminds me of Jesus' statement, "Blessed are they that mourn; for they shall be comforted" (Matt. 5:4). Israel's mourning of true repentance is coming, but she will be comforted.

IV. THE SALVATION OF ISRAEL (v. 10a)

"I will pour upon the house of David, and upon the inhabitants of Jerusalem, the Spirit of grace and of supplications."

A. Stated

God's pouring forth of His Spirit is the evidence of salvation because He never gives His Spirit to unbelievers (Rom. 8:9). The Holy Spirit is identified as the "Spirit of grace" (cf. Heb. 10:29) because was He given out of grace, and the Spirit "of supplication" because God's grace toward the remnant will result in repentant prayer. Zechariah is saying that just as God pours out refreshing showers on thirsty and parched ground, so will He pour out the Spirit of grace and supplication on repentant, needy Israel.

B. Supported

Joel prophesied essentially the same thing when he said, "It shall come to pass afterward, that I will pour out my Spirit upon all flesh, and your sons and daughters shall prophesy, your old men shall dream dreams, your young men shall see visions; and, also, upon the servants and upon the handmaids in those days will I pour out my Spirit" (Joel 2:28-29). That prophecy will be completely fulfilled at the second coming of Christ. Peter cited it at the birth of the church on the Day of Pentecost (Acts 2:15-21), but then the church was getting only a taste of it. Joel's prophecy is similar to Ezekiel's saying that God would replace Israel's stony heart with a heart of flesh and would put His Spirit within them (Ezek. 36:26-27).

Israel's repentance happens only because "they shall look upon [Him] whom they have pierced." Because God is speaking in first person in verse 10 as the One who was pierced—whom we know to be Christ—we not only have an affirmation of the deity of Christ but also an implication of the Trinity as the perspective shifts from the first Person to the third Person in the phrase "they shall look upon me whom they have pierced, and they shall mourn for him." There God sees Himself—as well as the incarnate Son of God—as the object of Israel's attention.

Don't let anyone tell you that Jesus is less than God or that the Jewish people weren't responsible at least in part for His death. God tells Israel that it was He in the Person of His Son whom they pierced. They may have used a Roman spear and a cross (John 19:34), but it was the plotting of their religious leaders that put Him there. Yet God in His great mercy can forgive anything—even the murder of His Messiah.

Conclusion

Zechariah 13:1 reiterates the promise of salvation for Israel: "In that day there shall be a fountain opened to the house of David and to the inhabitants of Jerusalem for sin and for uncleanness." God is going to wash away the sins of the nation. When they see Jesus and cry out, "My Lord and my God," they will realize it was the God of Israel whom they pierced. And then God will turn on the fountain of spiritual cleansing and wash His people clean as He pours out His Spirit.

In any age, repentance like that—true, honest repentance—will lead to spiritual cleansing. The fountain is open today. The apostle Paul said, "Now is the day of salvation" (2 Cor. 6:2). While we as Christians look expectantly to the day of national mourning and blessing for Israel, meanwhile we can tell every Jew and Gentile that they don't need to wait until then, because the fountain of salvation is open right now.

Focusing on the Facts

1. What is one reason Israel has drawn the attention of the world (see p. 86)?

2. What is a primary reason for Israel's reappearance as a nation (see p. 86)?
3. What will happen to Israel's tragic history on the day of her future political and spiritual victory (see p. 86)?
4. What is the future world war, which will include a siege of Jerusalem, commonly called (see p. 87)?
5. What are two reasons the nations of the world will converge on Israel during the Tribulation (see p. 87)?
6. Upon whom does the prophecy of Zechariah 12 focus (see p. 87)?
7. What does God's use of the first person in Zechariah 12 signify? What confidence does it provide (see pp. 87-88)?
8. What will happen to the nations that lay siege against Jerusalem (see p. 89)?
9. In prophetic literature, to what does the phrase "in that day" usually refer (see p. 89)?
10. Although Satan will entice the nations to come against Israel, with whose plan is that in accord (see p. 90)?
11. Identify the four armies present at the Battle of Armageddon (see pp. 90-91).
12. How will God begin His shielding of Israel, according to verse 4 (see p. 92)?
13. What will the governors of Judah turn from and to as their resource during the invasion of Israel (see p. 93)?
14. What will enable Jerusalem to "be inhabited again in her own place" (v. 6; see pp. 93-94)?
15. Why will God first deliver the inhabitants outside of Jerusalem (see p. 94)?
16. During the siege of Jerusalem, whom are its inhabitants compared to and why (v. 8; see p. 94)?
17. What will God do to the armies that attack Jerusalem at the end of the Tribulation (v. 9; see p. 95)?
18. Whom will Israel look upon as their victor? Why will that be a cause of mourning (vv. 10-14; see pp. 95-96)?
19. What's the one sin a person must repent of to be saved (see p. 96)?
20. What effect will the contrition of the aristocratic and privileged families of Israel have on the rest of the people (see pp. 96-97)?
21. What will God pour upon the faithful remnant of Israel? What does that indicate (v. 10; see pp. 97-98)?
22. What doctrines concerning God and Christ are implied in verse 10 (see p. 98)?

1. Before declaring that He would protect Israel, the Lord identified Himself as the One "who stretcheth forth the heavens, and layeth the foundation of the earth, and formeth the spirit of man within him" (Zech. 12:1). That is precisely the assurance Israel will need when faced with seemingly unbeatable odds. When you encounter trials, do you acknowledge God's power as the Creator of the universe and the One who gave us life? Memorize Jeremiah 32:17, which says, "Ah Lord God! Behold, Thou hast made the heavens and the earth by Thy great power and by Thine outstretched arm! Nothing is too difficult for Thee" (NASB). When you face obstacles that appear insurmountable, recall that verse and look at things from the perspective of the Creator of the universe.

2. Israel's recognition of Christ as her Messiah at the end of the Tribulation is one of the most dramatic examples of repentance in the Bible. Consequently Zechariah 12 is a wonderful chapter to share with your Jewish friends, relatives, neighbors, or co-workers. Rather than being someone they might assume to be indifferent or antagonistic toward the Jewish people, you have the opportunity to demonstrate that you believe the God of Abraham, Isaac, and Jacob will fulfill His promises to His people. Pray that you might lead them to mourn over their rejection of their Messiah and be comforted by the One who has opened a fountain of salvation for anyone who will repent of the sin of unbelief and turn to Jesus Christ. Not only may your words provide a sense of hope for them, but they will also let them know that God has not forgotten Israel but plans to make that nation the victorious focal point of the world.

7
The Cleansing of Israel

Outline

Introduction
A. The Patience of the Redeemer
   1. His people
   2. His preparation
   3. His perplexity
B. The Parable of Rejection
   1. The rejected servants
   2. The rejected son
   3. The rejected Stone
C. The Promise of Restoration
D. The Product of Repentance
   1. Micah 7:18-19
   2. Psalm 103:12-14
   3. Jeremiah 31:34
   4. Acts 3:19

Lesson
 I. Cleansing from the Defilement of Sin (v. 1)
    A. The Need of the Nation
    B. The Character of the Cleansing
    C. The Delineation of the Defilement
    D. The Forgiveness of the Faithful
 II. Cleansing from the Deception of Spurious Prophets (vv. 2-6)
    A. Exterminated (v. 2)
    B. Executed (v. 3)
    C. Embarrassed (v. 4)
    D. Exposed (vv. 5-6)
III. Cleansing Through the Death of the Shepherd (v. 7a)
    A. The Design of God
    B. The Deity of Christ

Introduction

There's a wonderful day coming for Israel. Zechariah identifies it as a day of spiritual cleansing. He said, "In that day there shall be a fountain opened to the house of David and to the inhabitants of Jerusalem for sin and for uncleanness" (Zech. 13:1).

A. The Patience of the Redeemer

Isaiah 5 tells us why Israel needs to be cleansed.

1. His people

In verse 1 the Lord refers to Israel as a vineyard: "Now will I sing to my well-beloved a song of my beloved touching his vineyard. My well-beloved hath a vineyard in a very fruitful hill." God (the "well beloved") planted a vineyard (Israel) on "a very fruitful hill" (Canaan).

2. His preparation

Verse 2 says, "He dug it, and gathered out the stones, and planted it with the choicest vine, and built a tower in the midst of it, and also made a winepress in it; and he looked for it to bring forth grapes, and it brought forth wild [inedible] grapes." God prepared a place for His people in Canaan, waiting for them to become what He desired. But instead they became as useless as wild grapes.

3. His perplexity

In verses 3-7 God says, "Inhabitants of Jerusalem, and men of Judah, judge, I pray you, between me and my vineyard. What could have been done more to my vineyard, that I have not done in it? Why, when I looked for it to bring forth grapes, brought it forth wild grapes? And now, I will tell you what I will do to my vineyard: I will take away its hedge [protection], and it shall be eaten up; and break down its wall, and it shall be trampled down. And I will lay it waste; it shall not be pruned, nor digged, but there shall come up briers and thorns; I will also command the clouds that they rain no rain upon it. For the vineyard of the Lord of hosts is the house of Israel, and the men of Judah his pleasant plant; and he looked for justice, but behold oppression; for righteousness, but behold a cry."

When the vineyard God planted rebelled and brought forth wild grapes, He promised to judge it by removing His protection and care. God promised to judge Israel because of their unbelief and rebellion.

B. The Parable of Rejection

Jesus tells a similar tragic parable in Matthew 21.

1. The rejected servants

Verse 33 says, "There was a certain householder, who planted a vineyard, and hedged it round about, and dug a winepress in it, and built a tower, and leased it to tenant farmers, and went into a far country." The householder is God. The vineyard is His kingdom. The farmers are the religious leaders of Israel, who were entrusted with the responsibility of teaching His truth.

Verses 34-36 say that "when the time of the fruit drew near, [the householder] sent his servants to the farmers, that they might receive the fruits of it. And the farmers took his servants, and beat one, and killed another, and stoned another. Again, he sent other servants more than the first; and they did the same unto them." The servants are the prophets that Israel refused to listen to. Jesus said, "O Jerusalem, Jerusalem, thou . . . killest the prophets, and stonest them who are sent unto thee" (Matt. 23:37).

103

2. The rejected son

Verses 37-39 say, "But last of all he sent unto them his son, saying, They will reverence my son. But when the farmers saw the son, they said among themselves, This is the heir; come, let us kill him and let us seize on his inheritance. And they caught him, and cast him out of the vineyard, and slew him." Jesus then asked the religious leaders, "When the lord, therefore, of the vineyard cometh, what will he do unto those farmers?" (v. 40). They answered, "He will miserably destroy those wicked men, and will lease his vineyard unto other farmers, who will render him the fruits in their seasons" (v. 41).

3. The rejected Stone

Jesus then replied, "Did ye never read in the scriptures, The stone which the builders rejected, the same is become the head of the corner; this is the Lord's doing, and it is marvelous in our eyes? Therefore say I unto you, The kingdom of God shall be taken from you, and given to a nation bringing forth the fruits of it. And whosoever shall fall on this stone shall be broken, but on whomsoever it shall fall, it will grind him to powder. And when the chief priests and Pharisees had heard his parables, they perceived that he spoke of them. But when they sought to lay hands on him, they feared the multitude, because they regarded him as a prophet" (vv. 42-46). The Jewish leaders might have fulfilled the parable right there and then by killing Jesus, but they feared the crowd.

God planted a vineyard—His kingdom—and entrusted it to the teachers and leaders of Israel. But when they were held accountable by the prophets He sent, they persecuted the prophets. And when God sent His own Son, whom they should have respected, they ultimately rejected Him and had Him killed. Therefore God took His kingdom away from them and gave it to those who would bring forth fruit, namely the church. Just as Isaiah indicted the nation for its failure to live up to God's standards, so Jesus indicted the leaders for their sins.

C. The Promise of Restoration

However, that parable does not indicate that God is finished with Israel. In Romans 11 He informs us that the church is like a branch from a wild olive tree grafted into the natural olive tree of the Abrahamic covenant of blessing. Referring to the Gentile church, Paul says, "If thou wert cut out of the olive tree which is wild by nature, and were grafted contrary to nature into a good olive tree, how much more shall these, who are the natural branches [Israel], be grafted into their own olive tree? . . . And so all Israel shall be saved" (Rom. 11:24, 26). The time is coming when God will put that natural branch back in the tree.

D. The Product of Repentance

God isn't through with His vineyard Israel. Although Isaiah and Jesus made clear God's attitude toward rebellious people, our God is also a forgiving God. He will cleanse Israel and restore her to her place of blessing.

1. Micah 7:18-19—Micah wrote, "Who is a God like unto thee, who pardoneth iniquity, and passeth by the transgression of the remnant of his heritage? He retaineth not his anger forever, because he delighteth in mercy. He will turn again; he will have compassion on us; he will subdue our iniquities; and thou wilt cast all their sins into the depths of the sea." All that Israel did in the past to the prophets and to God's Son will be forgiven.

2. Psalm 103:12-14—The psalmist said, "As far as the east is from the west, so far hath he removed our transgressions from us. As a father pitieth his children, so the Lord pitieth them that fear him. For he knoweth our frame; he remembereth that we are dust."

3. Jeremiah 31:34—"They shall all know me, from the least of them unto the greatest of them, saith the Lord; for I will forgive their iniquity, and I will remember their sin no more."

4. Acts 3:19—Peter said, "Repent, therefore, and be converted, that your sins may be blotted out." Forgiveness

is available to anyone who repents of his sins and turns to God.

God is a God of forgiveness. He throws our sins into the depths of the sea, removes them as far as the east is from the west, blots them out, and forgets them. God's unchangeable nature will override the seriousness of the sin of rejecting the Messiah. That is the message of Zechariah 13, where God promises to cleanse and forgive Israel.

Lesson

I. CLEANSING FROM THE DEFILEMENT OF SIN (v. 1)

"In that day there shall be a fountain opened to the house of David and to the inhabitants of Jerusalem for sin and for uncleanness."

A. The Need of the Nation

"In that day" refers to the day of the Lord, which is when Christ returns and Israel repents. "The house of David and . . . the inhabitants of Jerusalem" shows the totality of cleansing: it will affect royalty and commoners. The fountain of forgiveness will cleanse the people of Israel from the defilement of sin. Such forgiveness is the supreme need of Jew and Gentile alike. Every person is a sinner in God's eyes. The apostle Paul said, "There is none righteous, no, not one. . . . all have sinned, and come short of the glory of God" (Rom. 3:10, 23).

Israel has been defiled by its historic disobedience to the law of God and her outright rejection of Jesus Christ, the Messiah. In Romans 10:3 the apostle Paul says that "they, being ignorant of God's righteousness, and going about to establish their own righteousness, have not submitted themselves unto the righteousness of God." Israel prefered to create a system of works rather than follow the system of faith and grace that God ordained. In that state of unbelief, Israel remains guilty before God. In fact the people have committed the greatest sin of all: rejecting Christ.

106

B. The Character of the Cleansing

But what happens in the day of their repentance is wonderful. Israel will be cleansed with a fountain of forgiveness. The Hebrew word translated "fountain" (*maqor*) refers to a spring of water, but it is often used symbolically to refer to God as "the fountain of living waters" (Jer. 2:13; 17:13). Psalm 36:9 says, "With thee is the fountain of life." The fountain in Zechariah 13:1 is not used as the source of life or refreshment but as a means of cleansing and purification. God is going to cleanse Israel of all her filthiness.

The use of the Hebrew word translated "opened" conveys the idea of a continuous, permanent opening. The fountain Zechariah mentions will be a source of perennial purification. The fountain of cleansing was opened at the cross of Calvary, and it's been purifying souls ever since. Yet Israel as a whole has never been purified by it because of its unbelief and hardness of heart. But that will change when the people of Israel come to their Messiah in repentance. They will begin to experience what Christians have been experiencing for more than two thousand years—the perennial cleansing of Christ's death and resurrection. First John 1:7 says, "The blood of Jesus Christ . . . cleanseth us from all sin." The present-tense verb carries the idea of a continuing cleansing. As long as there is sin, there will be cleansing for the one who believes.

C. The Delineation of the Defilement

The Hebrew word translated "sin" (*chattath*) refers to that which misses the mark or goes the wrong way. It refers to a sin against man or God—an act of disobedience, indifference, or rebellion. The Hebrew word translated "uncleanness" identifies something to be shunned. In the book of Leviticus it is used to refer to ceremonial impurity such as occurred when an Israelite touched a dead body.

Israel will be cleansed of its moral and ceremonial defilement. Everyone needs that kind of cleansing because everyone is defiled. When Solomon dedicated the Temple, he said, "There is no man who sinneth not" (1 Kings 8:46). David said, "The Lord looked down from heaven upon the children of men, to see if there were any that did understand, and seek God. They are all gone aside, they are all together become filthy; there is none that doeth good, no, not one" (Ps. 14:2-3; cf. Rom. 3:11-12).

D. The Forgiveness of the Faithful

We are cleansed from our sin when we place our faith in the One who was pierced on the cross to pay the penalty for our sins and reconcile us to God. By believing in Him and receiving Him as your Savior, that cleansing can be applied to you.

Israel will one day experience that cleansing nationally. The people will again enjoy a covenantal relationship with God. Only the blood of Christ can provide that. Hebrews 9:13-14 says, "If the blood of bulls and of goats, and the ashes of an heifer sprinkling the unclean, sanctifieth to the purifying of the flesh, how much more shall the blood of Christ, who through the eternal Spirit offered himself without spot to God, purge your conscience from dead works to serve the living God?" Only the sacrifice of Christ purges the sinner's conscience and transforms his life so that he can willingly serve God.

II. CLEANSING FROM THE DECEPTION OF SPURIOUS PROPHETS (vv. 2-6)

The two besetting sins of Israel have always been idolatry and false prophecy. Wherever idolatry existed, it was the result of false prophets propagating it. But when Christ returns and cleanses Israel from its defilement, He is also going to cleanse the nation from the deception of those false prophets.

A. Exterminated (v. 2)

"It shall come to pass, in that day, saith the Lord of hosts, that I will cut off the names of the idols out of the land, and they shall no more be remembered; and also I will cause the prophets and the unclean spirit to pass out of the land."

Behind false prophecy is an unclean spirit. Psalm 96:5 says, "All the gods of the nations are idols." And Paul tells us that "the things which the Gentiles sacrifice, they sacrifice to demons" (1 Cor. 10:20). Behind false prophets and idols (who are thought to be gods) are unclean spirits.

"The unclean spirit" is not a pervading principle but an active agency that stands in direct contrast to "the Spirit of grace and of supplications" (Zech. 12:10). The agency of salvation is God's Spirit of grace, but the agency of idolatry is false prophets, demons, and Satan himself. The wicked spirits who energize false prophets are unclean because they drive their victims into moral impurities and false religion.

B. Executed (v. 3)

"It shall come to pass that, when any shall yet prophesy, then his father and his mother who begot him shall say unto him, Thou shalt not live; for thou speakest lies in the name of the Lord; and his father and his mother who begot him shall thrust him through when he prophesieth."

After Israel has been cleansed, anyone who tries to prophesy as a false prophet will be killed, even by those who are closely related to him. A mother and father will put their own child to death because they'll have such a hatred of false prophecy, it will overrule normal human feelings. They'll be the first to condemn the apostate to death.

C. Embarrassed (v. 4)

"It shall come to pass, in that day, that the prophets shall be ashamed, every one, of his vision, when he hath prophesied; neither shall they wear a rough garment to deceive."

Anyone who is a false prophet when Christ returns will be so ashamed that he won't want to be known as a prophet or even appear as one. The rough garment became the sign of a prophet from the days of Elijah, who was known for wearing a rough garment (1 Kings. 19:13, 19). It was either a goatskin or a piece of clothing woven out of camel's hair. False prophets will fear being identified as deceivers, so they'll deny any association whatsoever with prophecy.

D. Exposed (vv. 5-6)

"But he shall say, I am no prophet, I am a farmer; for man taught me to keep cattle from my youth. And one shall say unto him, What are these wounds in thine hands? Then he shall answer, Those with which I was wounded in the house of my friends [Heb., *ahavay,* "lovers"]."

In the day of Israel's cleansing, false prophets will deny being prophets and claim to have been farmers all their lives. When they denounce any association with pagan practices, others will challenge them to explain the wounds on their bodies. "Wounds in thine hands" could refer to anywhere on the arms or hands, or even across the torso. Pagans would cut themselves as part of their religious practice. When confronted with the question, the false prophet will have to admit that his wound came from his lovers. Commentator H. C. Leupold identifies those lovers as the idols that the false prophets were in love with (*Exposition of Zechariah* [Grand Rapids: Baker, 1956], p. 249). The self-inflicted wounds from their idolatries will give them away.

III. CLEANSING THROUGH THE DEATH OF THE SHEPHERD (v. 7a)

"Awake, O sword, against my shepherd, and against the man who is my fellow, saith the Lord of hosts; smite the shepherd."

The Spirit of God now contrasts the true Shepherd with the false shepherds, just described as being wounded by their idolatry. Not only will Israel be saved *from* something (idolatry), but *through* something as well—the death of the Shepherd. He's just as much a part of Israel's cleansing as anything. In fact, Israel couldn't be cleansed from the defilement of sin and the deception of false prophets apart from the Shepherd's death. God is speaking about the death of Christ, the good Shepherd, and the judgment therefore rendered upon sin.

A. The Design of God

The death of Jesus Christ was in the plan of God. He called for the sword to strike the Messiah, His "fellow." Jewish people for centuries have pleaded not to be blamed for the death of Christ. But such justification is unnecessary since God Himself takes the responsibility. The hatred of Satan, the fury of the chief priests, the contempt of Herod, and the cowardice of Pilate merely accomplished what God had designed to do from the very beginning—before the foundation of the world (1 Pet. 1:18-20).

B. The Deity of Christ

The Hebrew word translated "man" is an uncommon word. It refers to a strong man, not to an ordinary man. "Fellow" refers to a close associate. God identifies Christ as the mighty man of His union. A proper translation of verse 7 could be: "the mighty man who is coequal with Me." It is an affirmation of the deity of Jesus Christ, the mighty Shepherd who is God's equal (cf. Phil. 2:6). It is prophetic of Jesus' statement, "I and my Father are one" (John 10:30). Jesus is God. Micah could not have said the Messiah's "goings forth have been from of old, from everlasting" (Mic. 5:2), nor could Isaiah identify Him as "the mighty God" (Isa. 9:6), or Jeremiah call Him "the Lord Our Righteousness" (Jer. 23:5-6) unless the Messiah was equal to God.

IV. CLEANSING FROM THE DISPERSION OF THE SHEEP (v. 7b)

"The sheep shall be scattered [lit., "broken in pieces"]; and I will turn mine hand upon the little ones."

A. The Scattering Fulfilled

Not only were the disciples scattered after Christ was smitten, but the nation was as well. On the night He was betrayed, Jesus quoted Zechariah 13:7, saying, "I will smite the shepherd, and the sheep of the flock will be scattered abroad" (Matt. 26:31). When Jesus was arrested, the first to be scattered were His disciples. But He predicted a greater scattering, which occurred in A.D. 70 when Titus conquered Israel. The whole nation—leaderless and confounded, having spurned their Messiah—was scattered all over the world. In a sense God will cleanse Israel from their dispersion when He regathers them. It's exciting to be living in a time when we can begin to see that happening in preparation for the final regathering.

B. The Suffering Foretold

I believe the phrase "I will turn mine hand upon the little ones" refers to the persecution of the Jewish and Gentile believers in the early church. By Acts 5 there may have been twenty thousand Jewish believers in the Jerusalem church. And there are still Jewish people being saved today. I believe these "little ones" are the same as the "poor of the flock" in Zechariah 11:7, whom God turned His hand upon. The turning of God's hand refers to chastening and judgment (Ps. 81:14-15; Isa. 1:25; Ezek. 38:12; Amos 1:8). One of the first things the early church experienced was persecution. Acts 9:1 says that Paul before His conversion was "breathing out threatenings and slaughter against the disciples" (cf. 8:1). Just after Jesus made wonderful promises to His disciples about enabling them to bear spiritual fruit and receive His Spirit, He said, "If the world hate you, ye know that it hated me before it hated you. . . . If they have persecuted me, they will also persecute you. . . . They shall put you out of the synagogues; yea, the time cometh, that whosoever killeth you will think that he doeth God service" (John 15:18, 20; 16:2).

The message is simple: The good Shepherd would die for the sins of His people, who would be scattered because they rejected Him. And God would allow even those who were faithful to go through suffering and persecution so that the church might be pure. In the day of cleansing, God will completely regather His scattered flock.

V. CLEANSING FROM THE DEVASTATION OF SLAUGHTER (vv. 8-9a)

"It shall come to pass that in all the land, saith the Lord, two parts in it shall be cut off and die; but the third shall be left in it. And I will bring the third part through the fire, and will refine them as silver is refined, and will test them as gold is tested."

The Battle of Armageddon will be a terrible slaughter. Zechariah prophesies that it will take the lives of two-thirds of the people of Israel. Some do not take that figure literally since Isaiah mentions a tenth being spared (Isa. 6:13). But clearly the majority of the people of Israel will die, and only a portion will survive the Battle of Armageddon. The Antichrist and the armies of the world will attempt to wipe out the entire nation, but they will fail. The remaining third will be the believing remnant who look upon Christ in repentance at His return (Zech. 12:10) and will include the 144,000 mentioned in Revelation 7:4. They are the survivors whose hearts were prepared and who enter the earthly kingdom in their physical bodies. The Tribulation will be an unprecedented refining process for the nation of Israel.

VI. CLEANSING THROUGH THE DECISION OF THE SOUL (v. 9b)

"They shall call on my name, and I will hear them. I will say, It is my people; and they shall say, The Lord is my God."

The cleansing of Israel is a sovereign act of God, but it occurs in concert with the will of the people of Israel. God does not sovereignly redeem His people apart from their faith in Him. The people that were "not my people" (Heb., *lo ammi*) will become "my people" (Heb., *ammi*), according to God's prophecy in Hosea 1:9-11. From the midst of their fiery ordeal the remnant of Israel will see Jesus Christ and will call upon Him as their Lord. Their decision will consummate their cleansing. Isaiah said, "The ransomed of the Lord shall return, and come to Zion with songs and everlasting joy upon their heads; they shall obtain joy and gladness, and sorrow and sighing shall flee away" (Isa. 35:10). What a blessed consummation!

Our God is a forgiving God who will forgive His people Israel even though they descended from those who killed His Son. Because we are sinners, we need a God who can take away our sin. The fountain is open for all who will come. There is no need to wait.

Focusing on the Facts

1. In Isaiah's parable of the vineyard, why was God seemingly perplexed (Isa. 5:3-4; see pp. 102-3)?
2. How did God promise to judge Israel for her rebellion (Isa. 5:5-6; see p. 103)?

3. In Jesus' parable of the householder, identify the servants and the farmers. How did the farmers treat the servants (Matt. 21:33-36; see p. 103)?

4. What did the chief priests and Pharisees who heard the parable conclude that the lord would do after the farmers had killed his son? How did they react to Jesus' parable? Why (Matt. 21:41-46; see p. 104)?

5. To whom did Israel forfeit the kingdom? Does that mean that God is finished with Israel? Support your answer with Scripture (see p. 105).

6. What will allow Israel to be restored to her place of blessing? Support your answer with Scripture (see pp. 105-6).

7. Is spiritual cleansing needed only by Israel? Support your answer with Scripture (see p. 106).

8. What relationship did Israel have to God's righteousness, according to Romans 10:3 (see p. 106)?

9. What is the greatest sin Israel remains guilty of (see p. 106)?

10. Describe the fountain that will be opened to Israel (see p. 107).

11. Explain how cleansing from sin takes place today (see p. 107).

12. What alone can purge the sinner's conscience? What will that purging result in (see p. 108)?

13. Identify the two besetting sins of Israel and the source of each (see p. 108).

14. What do those sins drive their victims into (see p. 109)?

15. What will happen to false prophets after Israel has been cleansed (vv. 3-5; see pp. 109-10)?

16. Who ultimately takes responsibility for the death of Christ? Explain (1 Pet. 1:18-20; see pp. 110-11).

17. What does verse 7 imply about the nature of the smitten shepherd? List some Scripture references that explicitly teach the same thing (see p. 111).

18. At what times were the sheep of the smitten shepherd dispersed (see p. 111)?

19. Whom did God say He would "turn His hand upon"? What did Jesus say to confirm that reality (v. 7; see p. 112)?

20. Who will survive the Battle of Armageddon (vv. 8-9; see pp. 112-13)?

21. As a result of their spiritual refining, what will those survivors do and say (v. 9; see p. 113)?

22. Will the cleansing of Israel be purely a sovereign act of God? Explain (see p. 113).

Pondering the Principles

1. Divine forgiveness is a precious commodity. It is as necessary to us as air. Without it we would be eternally separated from God and trapped with unresolvable guilt in this life. Are you sensitive to the sins you commit against man and God? Are you quick to confess them and restore a right relationship with both? Meditate on Micah 7:18. Take a moment to praise the Lord that He "is faithful and righteous to forgive us our sins and to cleanse us from all unrighteousness" as we confess our sins to Him (1 John 1:9, NASB). Pray you might have an opportunity to tell that great truth to someone this week, giving him hope of forgiveness no matter how serious the sin.

2. Zechariah 13 affirms that God uses suffering in the lives of His people. In doing so He desires not only to purge false believers but also to strengthen the true believers. Jesus and the New Testament writers guaranteed that believers would encounter suffering (John 15:18, 20; 2 Tim. 3:12). When you experience it, do you joyfully accept it as part of God's purpose in your life (James 1:2-4)? If you are currently suffering or know someone who is, pray that you will develop great spiritual strength and trust in our faithful Lord, who has compassion on us and a deep awareness of our human frailties (Ps. 103:14).

8
The Day of the Lord

Outline

Introduction

Lesson
I. The Coming of the Day of the Lord (vv. 1-8)
   A. Declared (v. 1)
      1. The time
      2. The treasure
      3. The taunting
   B. Described (vv. 2-8)
      1. The gathering by God (v. 2a)
      2. The assault of the armies (v. 2b)
      3. The return of the Redeemer (vv. 3-8)
         a) His defense (v. 3a)
         b) His descent (vv. 4-8)
            (1) Its place (v. 4a)
            (2) Its product (v. 4b)
               (a) Supported
                  i) Nahum 1:5
                  ii) Micah 1:2-4
                  iii) Revelation 16:18-21
               (b) Stated
            (3) Its purpose (v. 5a)
            (4) It participants (v. 5b)
               (a) 1 Thessalonians 3:13
               (b) Colossians 3:4
               (c) Jude 14
            (5) Its peculiarity (vv. 6-8)
               (a) The appearance of the sky (v. 6)
                  i) Isaiah 13:9-10
                  ii) Revelation 6:12-14

Introduction

These are the last days of Israel's history as they are being regathered. They established their nation under a grant given to them by the United Nations providing international protection. Although the nation as a whole is still in a state of unbelief, they are being prepared for the day of their salvation, when they look on the One whom they once pierced. Prior to that time, they will make a pact with a false messiah, identified by Zechariah as a foolish shepherd and known to us as the Antichrist. Everything will take place peacefully during the first half of that seven-year covenant, but in the middle of it the Antichrist will break his covenant with Israel and require that they worship him alone. When the people of Israel refuse, he will gather the armies of the world to exterminate them. That attack, which will climax in a great siege of the city of Jerusalem, is known as the Battle of Armageddon.

It is precisely at the siege of Jerusalem that Zechariah 14 begins. Chapter 13 prophesies that the siege will begin successfully and bring about tremendous bloodshed and devastation. It will be an apparent victory for the Antichrist and his hosts. But just when his victory looks secure, Christ will return. Chapter 14 opens with a defeated Jerusalem, stripped of its possessions and honor, seemingly conquered by the world's armies. The conquerors are reveling in their spoils. However, Jesus' return completely reverses the tide of battle.

Lesson

I. THE COMING OF THE DAY OF THE LORD (vv. 1-8)

A. Declared (v. 1)

"Behold, the day of the Lord cometh, and thy spoil shall be divided in the midst of thee."

1. The time

The opening phrase "the day of the Lord cometh" is an announcement all by itself. You could almost put an exclamation mark at the end of it and start the next phrase as a new paragraph. The prophecy has now reached a climax identified as "the day of the Lord." It refers not to one day but to the period of time beginning with the rapture of the church extending through the millennial kingdom. That includes the Tribulation and the conquest and judgment of the nations when the Lord takes back the earth. It also includes the establishment of the kingdom and Christ's reign on earth for a thousand years, at the end of which Satan will be vanquished forever. Man's day of dominating the earth will end as the Lord establishes His reign.

2. The treasure

Chapter 14 begins with the siege of Jerusalem by the armies of the world. Prophecies in the books of Daniel and Revelation tell us four major armies will be gathered against Israel: the Soviet-Arab alliance from the north, the Egyptian-Arab alliance from the south, the revived Roman confederacy from the west, and the oriental confederacy from the east. They seem to have accomplished their goal of conquering Israel, because verse 1 says, "Thy spoil shall be divided in the midst of thee," referring to Jerusalem (indicated by the feminine pronoun personifying the city and its mention in the next verse).

3. The taunting

It was uncommon for an enemy to conquer a place and then divide the spoil in the midst of it; usually an army would haul it off. But those who successfully besiege Israel will have such a sense of victory and confidence, they will start divvying up the booty right there on the spot, as if to taunt the remaining inhabitants of Jerusalem. At that very moment, however, Jerusalem's extremity will become God's opportunity.

B. Described (vv. 2-8)

1. The gathering by God (v. 2a)

"I will gather all nations against Jerusalem to battle."

It may be a little surprising to Israel to learn that God Himself gathered the nations against Jerusalem. Their enemies are not pursuing their independent objectives or even solely accomplishing the will of Satan. God will use the Battle of Armageddon to purge the unbelieving from Israel and to judge the nations, just as Israel was used as an agency of judgment when it entered the Promised Land.

Revelation 16 indicates the means God will use to gather the armies to Jerusalem: "I saw three unclean spirits, like frogs, come out of the mouth of the dragon [Satan], and out of the mouth of the beast [the Antichrist], and out of the mouth of the false prophet. For they are the spirits of demons, working miracles, that go forth unto the kings of the earth and of the whole world, to gather them to the battle of that great day of God Almighty. . . . And he gathered them together into a place called in the Hebrew tongue Armageddon" (vv. 13-14, 16). Demons are going to gather rulers from all over the world to lead the great armies against Israel. But ironically those agencies of judgment will be judged themselves. The focal points of the battle will be Jerusalem and the plain of Megiddo in the north, although the battleground will extend throughout the land of Israel.

2. The assault of the armies (v. 2*b*)

"The city shall be taken, and the houses rifled, and the women ravished; and half of the city shall go forth into captivity, and the residue of the people shall not be cut off from the city."

Jeremiah 30:7 talks about "the time of Jacob's trouble," using Jacob as a metonym for the nation Israel. It refers to an unprecedented time of national calamity. The situation will seem beyond hope when the city is invaded, its houses plundered, its women raped, and half its inhabitants taken as prisoners of war. But God promises that "the residue" (the remnant or remainder) will be spared. I believe the half that is killed or taken away will be unbelievers and the surviving half will be the believing remnant, although it's difficult to say with certainty. Zechariah has already told us that two-thirds of the nation would perish, and now here we learn that half of the city of Jerusalem will perish. One reason believers will be spared is so that they can populate the earthly kingdom.

3. The return of the Redeemer (vv. 3-8)

a) His defense (v. 3*a*)

"Then shall the Lord go forth, and fight against those nations, as when he fought in the day of battle."

God is not about to allow the enemy to destroy those who are ready to put faith in the Messiah. They will be like those who were baptized by John the Baptist, a people prepared for His coming (Matt. 3:5-6). To prevent the eradication of that remnant, the Lord will personally intervene to fight against those nations. It will be "as when he fought in the day of battle." That is a general reference to Old Testament battles in which God fought for His people, such as with Joshua at Gibeon (Josh. 10:14), in the conquest of Canaan

(23:3), and in the defeat of Sisera (Judg. 4:15). Just as the Lord has fought for His people in the past, so He will do in the future. Like Joseph, who made himself known to his brothers in their hour of deepest distress, so will God come in the time of Jacob's trouble in the Person of the Lord Jesus Christ.

b) His descent (vv. 4-8)

(1) Its place (v. 4*a*)

"His feet shall stand in that day upon the Mount of Olives, which is before Jerusalem on the east."

When the Lord returns to deliver His people He will land on the Mount of Olives. That verse is a tremendous affirmation of the deity of Jesus Christ. In Acts 1:11 the angels told those who witnessed Christ's ascension to heaven that He would return to the same place (the Mount of Olives) in the same way (in a personal, visible form). I don't believe the mention of His return to that place is symbolic. Jesus will literally return to the Mount of Olives as Zechariah prophesied and the angels verified.

If Only the Mount of Olives Could Talk!

The Mount of Olives was where Jesus shed so many tears night after night, where He uttered so many of His prayers, and where He held many precious conversations with His disciples. It supported His weary feet as they walked its paths and witnessed the agony and bloodshed of His arrest and crucifixion, along with the exhilaration of His resurrection and ascension. What wonderful things it could tell us if it could talk! That same mountain will one day experience His return and receive those same feet.

(2) Its product (v. 4*b*)

"The Mount of Olives shall cleave in its midst toward the east and toward the west, and there shall be a very great valley; and half of the mountain shall remove toward the north, and half of it toward the south."

That will be a tremendous earthquake! Such seismic upheavals are not uncommon when God announces His coming in judgment.

(a) Supported

    i) Nahum 1:5—When the Lord comes in judgment "the mountains quake before him, and the hills melt, and the earth is burned at his presence, yea, the world and all that dwell in it."

    ii) Micah 1:2-4—"Hear, all ye peoples; hearken, O earth, and all that is in it; and let the Lord God be witness against you, the Lord from his holy temple. For, behold, the Lord cometh forth out of his place, and will come down, and tread upon the high places of the earth. And the mountains shall be melted under him, and the valleys shall be cleft, like wax before the fire, and like the waters that are poured down a steep place."

    iii) Revelation 16:18-21—The apostle John saw a vision of the final judgment upon the earth before Christ's return: "There were voices, and thunders, and lightnings; and there was a great earthquake, such as was not since men were upon the earth, so mighty an earthquake, and so great. And the great city was divided into three parts, and the cities of the nations fell; and great Babylon came in remembrance before God, to give unto her the cup of the wine of the fierceness of his wrath. And every island fled away, and the mountains were not found. And there fell upon men great hail out of

123

heaven, every stone about the weight of a talent [one hundred pounds]." A supernatural earthquake will generate a worldwide cataclysm.

(b) Stated

When the feet of Jesus Christ touch down on the Mount of Olives at His return, there will be a tremendous release of power. It will be very different from His quiet first coming as a baby born in a stable. The world will know immediately that He has arrived, and many will scream for the rocks and the mountains to fall on them to hide them from His face, knowing the judgment He brings (Rev. 6:16).

One resulting phenomenon of this earthquake will be the creation of a valley running east and west as the mountain is pulled northward and southward. Although it offers some protection, the Mount of Olives is the greatest obstacle to an eastern escape from Jerusalem. But this large new valley going straight out from Jerusalem to the east will offer a quick route of escape for the besieged inhabitants of Jerusalem.

I believe that valley is "the Valley of Jehoshaphat," which Joel also calls "the valley of decision" (Joel 3:12, 14). That is where God will gather all the nations and judge them after His people have fled to safety. He will devastate the armies of the world as they attempt to pursue the remnant of Israel that will have just escaped eastward through the valley He created for that purpose. It will probably be similar to the judgment of Pharaoh's army as it tried to cross the sea God had opened up for Israel's escape from Egypt—God's judgment will come crashing down on them when the armies enter that mighty valley.

(3) Its purpose (v. 5a)

"Ye shall flee to the valley of the mountains; for the valley of the mountains shall reach unto Azel; yea, ye shall flee, as ye fled from before the earthquake in the days of Uzziah, king of Judah."

The Lord now calls the valley He just created "the valley of the mountains," for it was created when the Mount of Olives split in half. The valley shall reach unto "Azel [Heb., "be near to"]." In Zechariah's day there was apparently a place known by that name on the east side of Jerusalem. The implication is that the valley will begin near a gate to the city, thus providing a quick escape from it and preventing the need to run up and down any inclines to reach the valley.

"The earthquake in the days of Uzziah" is mentioned in Amos 1:1, but we don't know anything more about it. Apparently it was a terrible earthquake that caused the people of Jerusalem to flee the city. The flight at the Lord's return will be like that of King Uzziah's day.

(4) It participants (v. 5b)

"The Lord, my God, shall come, and all the saints with thee."

That is another great statement affirming the deity of Christ. The One whose feet will land on the Mount of Olives at His bodily, visible return is the same Lord called "the Lord, my God." And, as many New Testament verses indicate, He will be accompanied by the saints.

(a) 1 Thessalonians 3:13—Believers will be established unblamable in holiness "at the coming of our Lord Jesus Christ with all his saints." Paul was exhorting the Thessalonians to be spiritually ready for Christ's return.

(*b*) Colossians 3:4—Believers who have already gone to be with the Lord will be a part of that returning group of saints: "When Christ, who is our life, shall appear, then shall ye also appear with him in glory."

(*c*) Jude 14—Jude said, "Behold, the Lord cometh with ten thousands of his saints."

When Christ comes from heaven with all the saints dressed in white robes and riding on white horses (Rev. 19:14) is when I believe the remnant of Israel will look up and recognize the One whom they pierced and will mourn for Him as an only son (Zech. 12:10). That is when victory over the armies and the mourning and repentance of chapter 12 will take place and when the fountain of chapter 13 will be opened. What a fantastic day for the nation of Israel!

(5) Its peculiarity (vv. 6-8)

(*a*) The appearance of the sky (v. 6)

"It shall come to pass, in that day, that the light shall not be clear, nor dark."

When Jesus comes, the stars, the sun, and the moon will fade. Elsewhere Scripture mentions such changes in the heavens at the end times.

i) Isaiah 13:9-10—"The day of the Lord cometh, cruel both with wrath and fierce anger. . . . For the stars of heaven and the constellations thereof shall not give their light; the sun shall be darkened in its going forth, and the moon shall not cause its light to shine" (cf. Isa. 24:23; Joel 3:14-16; Matt. 24:29-30).

ii) Revelation 6:12-14—"The sun became black as sackcloth of hair, and the moon became like blood; and the stars of heav-

126

en fell unto the earth, even as a fig tree casteth her untimely figs, when she is shaken of a mighty wind. And the heaven departed as a scroll when it is rolled together."

In the midst of the blackness comes the blazing revelation of Jesus Christ with all His saints. At that moment Israel is going to look upon her Messiah in repentance and be wonderfully saved and gathered into the kingdom. The rest of the world will cry out in terror and be judged (Rev. 6:15-16).

(b) The arrival of the Savior (v. 7)

"But it shall be one day which shall be known to the Lord, not day, nor night; but it shall come to pass that, at evening time, it shall be light."

The Hebrew word translated "one" means "unique." That day will be like no other day. The laws of nature will go out of balance. Night and day will be suspended at that point. The light from the sun will be replaced by the light of Christ's blazing glory, which will fill the earth. He will arise as "the Sun of righteousness . . . with healing in his wings" (Mal. 4:2). There will be salvation for all who submit to that Light in faith but judgment for those who curse it.

(c) The alteration of the surroundings (v. 8)

"It shall be, in that day, that the living waters shall go out from Jerusalem; half of them toward the former sea, and half of them toward the hinder sea; in summer and in winter shall it be."

Jerusalem will be dramatically different. Right in the middle of Mount Moriah, where the Jerusalem Temple would have been, God will create a gushing spring that will send rivers to both the east and the west. I believe that it will be real water, because Isaiah says the desert will "blossom like the rose" (Isa. 35:1). A skeptic may doubt that there is water under the ground there, but the question is immaterial, because God can create water whenever He needs it. I also believe that the water is a prophetic picture of blessing flowing from Jerusalem, which will be the center of the kingdom.

II. THE CORONATION OF THE LORD AS KING (vv. 9-11)

A. The Primacy of the Potentate (v. 9)

"The Lord shall be king over all the earth; in that day shall there be one Lord, and his name one."

The first thing that happens after Christ arrives is His coronation. He'll be King not only in heaven but also on earth. His return to reign over an earthly kingdom is a promised reality.

There will be "one Lord, and his name one." That is, there will be only one religion in the entire world during the millennial kingdom. Christ, who will rule with a rod of iron (Rev. 19:15), will have done away with all false religions spawned by Satan. The world will worship our unique and incomparable Lord alone, the only wise God and Savior (1 Tim. 1:17; Jude 25), the Lord Jesus Christ.

B. The Prominence of the Palatial City (v. 10)

"All the land shall be turned like the Arabah from Geba to Rimmon south of Jerusalem; and it shall be lifted up, and inhabited in its place, from Benjamin's gate unto the place of the first gate, unto the corner gate, and from the tower of Hananel unto the king's winepresses."

When Christ comes in judgment upon the nations, the tremendous earthquake that takes place will create the valley running east, and Mount Moriah will be split open so that water starts to flow, allowing the entire land from Geba in the north to Rimmon in the south (a distance of about forty miles) to become like the Arabah. The Arabah is the longest, deepest, and flattest valley in the world. It runs from the Sea of Galilee southward beyond the Dead Sea, where it is as low as 1,300 feet below sea level. Zechariah is prophesying that all the mountainous terrain around Jerusalem will be as low as the Arabah. As a result, Jerusalem will stick up like a solitaire diamond on a ring.

Then God will rebuild the city of Jerusalem according to the dimensions given in verse 10. In its glory, before the nation's exile, the dimensions the city reached from the gates to the tower to the winepresses. Jerusalem won't be a small village as it was in Zechariah's time. It will be prominent in appearance and the royal city containing the throne of Jesus Christ. It will be exalted in both place and purpose.

C. The Peace Among the People (v. 11)

"Men shall dwell in it, and there shall be no more utter destruction; but Jerusalem shall be safely inhabited."

What an incredible day for Jerusalem—no more destruction, no more curse, no more idolatry, and no more apostasy! Not only will the Lord be crowned on that day, but the city of Jerusalem itself will be crowned and become the jewel of the earth.

III. THE CONQUEST OF THE NATIONS (vv. 12-15)

A. Its Elements (vv. 12-14a)

"This shall be the plague with which the Lord will smite all the peoples that have fought against Jerusalem: their flesh shall consume away while they stand upon their feet, and their eyes shall consume away in their holes [sockets], and their tongue shall consume away in their mouth. And it shall come to pass, in that day, that a great tumult from the Lord shall be among them; and they shall lay hold every one on the hand of his neighbor, and his hand shall rise up against the hand of his neighbor. And Judah also shall fight at Jerusalem."

Having seen the glorious results of our Lord's return, Zechariah now describes what will happen to the godless and how Israel will be able to gain the victory.

1. A deadly plague

   This plague will cause the nation's flesh, eyes, and tongues to rot while they are standing. Those who are judged will depart into everlasting punishment, while the believing remnant will hear Christ say, "Come, ye blessed of my Father, inherit the kingdom prepared for you" (Matt. 25:34).

2. A terrible confusion

   At some point during the Lord's judgment—and it's difficult to know the exact sequence of events—a "tumult" of confusion will result among the armies and cause them to slay themselves.

3. A superhuman strength

   While the enemies of Israel suffer, God will give His people great strength, thus enabling them to victoriously assist in the battle.

B. Its Effect (v. 14b)

   "The wealth of all the nations round about shall be gathered together—gold, and silver, and apparel—in great abundance."

   The tables will be turned immediately: instead of the nations counting all their booty acquired from Israel (v. 1), the wealth of all the nations will be gathered and brought into the hands of God's people.

C. Its Extent (v. 15)

   "So shall be the plague of the horse, of the mule, of the camel, and of the ass, and of all the beasts that shall be in these tents, as this plague."

The plague of destruction that afflicts God's enemies will even extend to their livestock.

IV. THE CHARACTER OF THE KINGDOM (vv. 16-21)

A. Its Worship of the Lord (vv. 16-19)

1. The pilgrimage (v. 16)

"It shall come to pass that every one that is left of all the nations which came against Jerusalem shall even go up from year to year to worship the King, the Lord of hosts, and to keep the feast of tabernacles."

I believe there will be a believing remnant from even the nations who turned to Christ at His coming or at some point during the Tribulation. Such believers will make an annual pilgrimage to Jerusalem to worship the Lord and keep the Feast of Tabernacles. That feast celebrates the time when God dwelt (Heb., *sakan*, "tabernacled") with Israel in the wilderness. And it will be celebrated in the future, for God, in the Person of His Son, will again dwell among His people.

2. The punishment (vv. 17-19)

a) An absence of rain (v. 17)

"It shall be that whoever will not come up of all the families of the earth unto Jerusalem to worship the King, the Lord of hosts, even upon them shall be no rain."

Nations who refuse to come to Jerusalem to worship Christ will experience a drought. Such a condition could result in disaster.

b) An affliction by plague (vv. 18-19)

"If the family of Egypt go not up, and come not, that have no rain, there shall be the plague, with which the Lord will smite the nations that come not up to keep the feast of tabernacles. This shall be the punishment of Egypt, and the punishment of all nations that come not up to keep the feast of tabernacles."

One nation that might not care about the absence of rain is Egypt. It hardly ever rains there, and the Nile River supplies all the water it needs. Such nations will be afflicted by a plague.

B. Its Way of Life (vv. 20-21)

"In that day shall there be upon the bells of the horses, holiness unto the Lord; and the pots in the Lord's house shall be like the bowls before the altar. Yea, every pot in Jerusalem and in Judah shall be holiness unto the Lord of hosts; and all they that sacrifice shall come and take of them, and boil in them; and in that day there shall be no more a Canaanite in the house of the Lord of hosts."

The phrase "holiness unto the Lord" was engraved on a gold plate attached to the high priest's turban. It signified that he was set apart from every other man. He had a uniquely holy function. There was no one like the high priest. Zechariah prophesied that everything—even mundane and ordinary things like the bells that decorate horses and common pots and pans—will be as holy as the high priest and the altar bowls once were to Israel in days past.

The promise that there will no longer be "a Canaanite in the house of the Lord" is a euphemistic way of saying that morally and spiritually unclean persons will be excluded from entering the millennial Temple. Before Israel conquered the Promised Land, the vile Canaanites inhabited it. The term Canaanite became proverbial in Israel for a morally degenerate person.

In the kingdom the whole world will be considered holy to the Lord. The Lord wants a holy people, and He has called His church to be holy. In Ephesians 5 the apostle Paul tells believing husbands, "Love your wives, even as Christ also loved the church, and gave himself for it, that he might sanctify and cleanse it . . . that he might present it to himself a glorious church, not having spot, or wrinkle, or any such thing; but that it should be holy and without blemish" (vv. 25-27). God wants a holy church and a holy people. And in that day He will have it!

Focusing on the Facts

1. Although the nation of Israel is being gathered by God while still in a state of unbelief, she is being prepared for what (see p. 118)?
2. What is the opening scene of Zechariah 14 (p. 119)?
3. What does "the day of the Lord" refer to (see p. 119)?
4. What will the seemingly victorious armies do in the midst of Jerusalem (v. 1; see p. 120)?
5. Explain God's objectives for bringing the nations against Israel. According to Revelation 16, what agency does He use to accomplish that (see p. 120)?
6. Although the battleground will probably cover the entire land of Israel, where will the focal points of the final battle be (see pp. 120-21)?
7. What will happen to Jerusalem when the siege is successful (v. 2)? Who might "the residue of the people" be (see p. 121)?
8. What will happen to protect those people (v. 3; see pp. 121-22)?
9. List other biblical victories in which the Lord played a decisive part (pp. 121-22).
10. Identify the place of the Lord's return to deliver His people, and give New Testament confirmation of that (see p. 122).
11. Describe what happens the moment the Lord touches ground (v. 4; see pp. 122-24).
12. Who will accompany the Lord at His return? Support your answer with Scripture (v. 5; see pp. 125-26).
13. What will happen to the appearance of the sky at Christ's second coming? What will those peculiar changes highlight (vv. 6-7; see pp. 126-27)?
14. What will the literal fountain in Jerusalem be symbolic of (v. 8; see pp. 127-28)?
15. Describe the religious focus in the millennial kingdom (v. 9; see p. 128).
16. Describe how the status of Jerusalem and the topography around it will be changed (v. 10; see pp. 128-29).

17. What are three elements that will play a part in the conquest of the nations (vv. 12-14; see p. 130)?
18. How will the tables be turned when the nations are conquered (v. 14; see p. 130)?
19. What will the believing remnant from the nations do on an annual basis in the Millennium? What will happen to those who fail to come (vv. 16-19; see pp. 131-32)?
20. How will life on earth in the kingdom be different from what it is now (vv. 20-21; see p. 132)?

Pondering the Principles

1. Christ is the theme of the book of Zechariah. In chapter 1 He is the Riding One. In chapter 2 He is the Measuring One. In chapter 3 He is the Cleansing One. In chapter 4 He is the Empowering One. In chapter 5 He is the Judging One. In chapter 6 He is the Crowned One. In chapter 7 He is the Rebuking One. In chapter 8 He is the Restoring One. In chapter 9 He is the Kingly One. In chapter 10 He is the Blessing One. In chapter 11 He is the Shepherding One. In chapter 12 He is the Returning One. In chapter 13 He is the Smitten One. In chapter 14 He is the Reigning One. Zechariah saw Christ. Did you catch his vision? Ezra 6:14 tells us that the people of Israel "prospered through the prophesying of . . . Zechariah." Have you? Now that you've completed this study, read the entire book of Zechariah straight through. Make sure you know the Christ Zechariah so looked forward to, and talk about Him to those around you.

2. God's purpose throughout history has been to show man that he is a sinner in need of a Savior. That theme will come to a climax at the return of Christ to judge the nations and deliver the believing remnant. Knowing that His goal is to establish a people "holy and blameless before Him" (Eph. 1:4, NASB), are you living your life in a way that reflects that noble goal? Meditate on 1 John 3:2-3 and 2 Peter 3:10-15. Commit yourself to being more sensitive to sin in your life and more willing to confess and repent of it. Seek now to be a holy example of the perfection we will experience in His kingdom.

Scripture Index

Topical Index